West Indian Poetry

An anthology for schools

KENNETH RAMCHAND
Senior Lecturer in English
University of the West Indies

CECIL GRAY
Senior Lecturer in Education
University of the West Indies

COVER ILLUSTRATION BY
KARL CRAIG

Longman Caribbean

Longman Caribbean Limited
Trinidad and Jamaica

Longman Group Limited
Longman House, Burnt Mill, Harlow,
Essex CM20 2JE, England
and Associated Companies throughout the World

First published 1972
Ninth impression 1984

ISBN 0 582 76707 5
Set in Monophoto Ehrhardt

Printed in Hong Kong by
Sing Cheong Printing Co. Ltd.

ACKNOWLEDGEMENTS

We are grateful to the following for permission to reproduce copyright material:
the author for 'Colonisation in Reverse' from *Jamaica Labrish*, by Louise Bennett; the author for 'The Visit', 'Mackerel', 'Drought', 'Soul on Ice' and 'Noah', by Wayne Brown, from *Breaklight* edited by Andrew Salkey; Jonathan Cape Ltd., for 'Le Loupgarou', 'In a Green Night', 'The Hurricane', 'A Lesson for this Sunday' and 'Allegre' from *In A Green Night* and 'The Falls' from the 'Guyana Sequence' from *The Gulf* by Derek Walcott; Andre Deutsch for 'An Old Jamaican Woman thinks about the Hereafter' from *On This Mountain* by A. L. Hendriks; the author for 'For Palinurus, the Lost Helmsman' from *Love Leaps Here* by John O. Figueroa; the author's estate for 'The Castaways', 'The Harlem Dancer' and 'I Shall Return' by Claude McKay from *The Selected Poems of Claude McKay*; the author for 'Tell me Tress: What are you Whispering?' by Wilson Harris from *Themes of Song* edited by A. J. Seymour; William Heinemann Ltd., for 'Bird' by Dennis Scott from *Young Commonwealth Poets '65*; the author for 'Sheep' by K. E. Ingram; the author for 'The Room' by Cliff Lashley; Lawrence & Wishart Ltd., for 'This is the Dark Time My Love', 'Till I Collect', 'Death of a Comrade', 'The Knife of Dawn' and an extract from 'Death of a Slave' from *Poems of Resistance* by Martin Carter; the author for 'Jaffo the Calypsonian' by I. A. McDonald; the author for 'The True Gage', 'Don' and 'Sammy' by Anthony McNeill; the author and Bim for 'The Pond' and 'The Castle', and the author and John Murray for 'To a Crippled Schoolmaster' by Mervyn Morris; the author and The Longman Group Ltd., for 'The Revolt of Chief Tacky' by Alma Norman; Oxford University Press for 'Columbus' from *Selected Poems* by Louis Simpson (this poem first appeared in 'The New Yorker' magazine), 'The Emigrants' (part 2), 'The Dust', and extract from 'New World A'Comin', 'South' from *Rights of Passage* by Edward Brathwaite, an extract from 'Leopard', 'Ancestors' and 'Ogun' from *Islands*, by Edward Brathwaite, 'Pelicans', 'The Lesson' from *A Tropical Childhood and Other Poems* by Edward Lucie-Smith; the author for 'Road Mending' by Barnabas J. Ramon-Fortuné from Caribbean Quarterly Vol. 5 No. 3; the author for 'Uncle Time', 'A Comfort of Crows', 'The Dumb-School Teacher' (first published in *Seven Jamaican Poets* – Bolivar Press, 1971), 'Cortège', 'Pages from a Journal, 1834' (first published in *Jamaica Journal* Vol. 3 No. 3 Sept 1969), and 'Squatter's Rites' by Dennis Scott; the author for 'There Runs a Dream' and 'Carrion Crows' from Kyk-over-al by A. J. Seymour; the author for 'These Golden Moments' and 'This Land' by M. G. Smith; we are unable to trace the copyright holder for 'High Noon' by Raymond Barrow from Caribbean Quarterly Vol. 5 No. 3 (1958); the author for

'Landscape Painter, Jamaica', 'History Lesson' and 'Kite Flying' by Vivian Virtue.

We have been unable to trace the copyright holders of the following and would be grateful for any information that would enable us to do so:

'The Cat' by W. Adolphe Roberts from *A Treasury of Jamaican Poetry* complied by J. E. Clare McFarlane; 'Henry's Ambition' from *Heights and Depths* by Una Marson; 'A Market Basket in the Car' and 'Now the Lignum-Vitae Blows' from *Orange Valley and Other Poems* by Tom Redcam; 'Hard Luck' from *Poems in All Moods* by Alfred M. Cruickshank.

Contents

Foreword

This anthology of West Indian poetry is intended for use at and above Fourth Form level in secondary schools anywhere. Some of the poems are probably also useful at a lower level, while a few may be somewhat difficult even for secondary school pupils; but we see that as advantageous for both teachers and pupils in the study of the growth of West Indian expression in verse, and more particularly in training young readers in how to read poems.

The commentaries at the end of the book attempt to chronicle in broad outline the development of West Indian art in verse, since an awareness of a growing tradition in West Indian literature seems, at this stage, to be especially valuable. But they are also to promote an understanding of the possible relationships between literary sophistication and perspectives, on the one hand, and the social changes in the region, on the other. It should, however, be clearly understood that the commentaries are not intended, and must not be allowed, to obstruct the operation of personal responses and observations on the part of the readers. For this reason they are placed last, after the poems.

The teacher, naturally, would want to acquaint himself with what is said in a commentary before exposing the pupils to the poems in the classroom, at least to see what he agrees with. But it cannot be over-stressed that in the classroom the poems should first be dealt with as poems before the general background commentary and evaluations are considered. For this central purpose we have suggested some questions for discussion of every poem. We are not implying that the questions we offer are the only ones that could be raised or touched upon. Indeed, we see it as inevitable that the discussion of any one question, one of ours or not, must involve discussion of several subsidiary matters both leading up to and arising from the main question.

It is to be remembered, too, that discussion must not descend into pointless dissection or, worse, desiccation. In every exposure of poems to pupils in a classroom, repeated oral readings—not memorization—of the poem and parts of the poem at appropriate times during the lesson must be an indispensable feature: if only to preserve the sense of the wholeness of the poem—the unity of impression and the feeling or feelings being communicated—and to assist in the revelation of connections of various kinds. The questions we have suggested to develop thinking and apprehension presuppose such constant readings aloud to retain the impact of the poem as a whole and to reveal certain relationships.

We ourselves would like to reveal here that in this anthology the selection, arrangement and commentaries were done by Kenneth Ramchand, and the questions for apprehension through thought and discussion were suggested by Cecil Gray.

KR
CG

Making

LANDSCAPE PAINTER, JAMAICA
for Albert Huie

I watch him set up easel,
Both straddling precariously
A corner of the twisted, climbing
Mountain track.

A tireless humming-bird, his brush
Dips, darts, hovers now here, now there,
Where puddles of pigment
Bloom in the palette's wild small garden.

The mountains pose for him
In a family group—
Dignified, self-conscious, against the wide blue screen
Of morning; low green foot-hills
Sprawl like grandchildren about the knees
Of seated elders. And behind them, aloof,
Shouldering the sky, patriarchal in serenity,
Blue Mountain Peak bulks.

And the professional gaze
Studies positions, impatiently waiting
For the perfect moment to fix
Their preparedness, to confine them
For the pleasant formality
Of the family album.

His brush a humming-bird
Meticulously poised . . .
The little hills fidgeting,
Changelessly changing,
Artlessly frustrating
The painter's art.

VIVIAN VIRTUE
b Jamaica, 1911

2

ROAD-MENDING

Patches of black
In the pitch
Make the most
Unusual patterns:
Irregular blocks,
Birds' wings,
Shapes of ships,
Animals' heads,
Curiously
Interfigured.

This is the
Road-mender's art:
With tar and gravel
To design
A dozen or more
Shapes and figures:
To figure out
From fancy only
How to inlay
Gravel and tar . . . . .

BARNABAS J. RAMON-FORTUNÉ
b Trinidad, 1917

from *Caribbean Quarterly*, Vol 5, No 3, 1958

DISCOVERER

Columbus from his after-
deck watched stars, absorbed in water,
melt in liquid amber drifting

through my summer air.
Now with morning, shadows lifting,
beaches stretched before him cold and clear.

Birds circled flapping flag and mizzen
mast: birds harshly hawking, without fear.
Discovery he sailed for was so near.

Columbus from his after-
deck watched heights he hoped for,
rocks he dreamed, rise solid from my simple water.

Parrots screamed. Soon he would touch
our land, his charted mind's desire.
The blue sky blessed the morning with its fire.

But did his vision
fashion, as he watched the shore,
the slaughter that his soldiers

furthered here? Pike
point and musket butt,
hot splintered courage, bones

cracked with bullet shot,
tipped black boot in my belly, the
whip's uncurled desire?

Columbus from his after-
deck saw bearded fig trees, yellow pouis
blazed like pollen and thin

waterfalls suspended in the green
as his eyes climbed towards the highest ridges
where our farms were hidden.

Now he was sure
he heard soft voices mocking in the leaves.
What did this journey mean, this

new world mean: dis-
covery? Or a return to terrors
he had sailed from, known before?

I watched him pause.

Then he was splashing silence.
Crabs snapped their claws
and scattered as he walked towards our shore.

EDWARD BRATHWAITE
b Barbados, 1930

Part 2 of 'The Emigrants', from *Rights of Passage*, Oxford, 1967

THESE GOLDEN MOMENTS

These golden moments
All flow out of pain
When next you hear my songs
Remember how
Only this singing like a sacrifice
Can keep me sane
And when you sing my songs
Remember too
How all the gold that flows
From this mad heart
Would not be gold at all
Apart from you
But the song silent
And the singer dead
And madness sitting
At the sacrifice.

M. G. SMITH
b Jamaica, 1921

Narrative Poems

HENRY'S AMBITION
A true incident

Little Henry was just ten and lived beside the sea.
You would think he was ambitious a sailor man to be,
But no, though he went fishing and rowing many a day,
His hopes for future happiness did hardly lie that way.

To none he told his secret, though often one would ask
If when he grew to manhood he would like a special task;
His large brown eyes grew larger but he never said a word,
And he kept it as a secret, so that nobody heard.

But out it came one morning in a most mysterious way,
The little man went fishing with his Uncle in the bay.
The sea was very angry and huge waves dashed about,
To hear each other speaking at length each had to shout.

A mighty wave above them rose, they had to sink or swim,
Poor Henry sank beneath the waves, his eyes with fright grew dim.
Full twice he rose and sank again when strong arms caught his waist
And bore him o'er the water; there was no time to waste.

With eyes shut tight, and sputtering mouth his Uncle heard him say,
'I cannot drive a motor-car yet I must drown to-day.'
And this was followed by a groan and consciousness then fled.
When next he opened his brown eyes he found himself in bed.

Today Henry to manhood grown can drive a motor car,
And never tires or makes a slip although the way be far.
He now has new ambitions, and I hope they will come true
As the cherished one he uttered when he thought his life was through.

UNA MARSON
b Jamaica, 1905–1965

from *Heights and Depths*, Gleaner Co Ltd, 1931

HARD LUCK

Sam Droggan, sure, had rotten luck
The night he stole his neighbour's duck;
For as he gained the open street,
Where stood a Bobby on the beat,
   'Quack!' said the duck.

They locked him in a lonely cell;
He sat, and then began to yell,
But not for long; for in he came,
The Sergeant with the dreaded name—
   'Twas Rough-house Joc!

Well, Droggan's skin was pretty sore
Next morning as he stood before
The Magistrate, to whom he said
'Your Worship, heaven strike me dead!
   I stole no duck!'

But when the evidence was heard
(The duck was there, but spoke no word)
His worship said: 'The case is clear;
I find you guilty. But, I fear,
   You had no luck.'

Now, Droggan's lawyer (honest, he
Resolved to labour for his fee)
Rose from his seat, inclined his head
And cleared his throat and suavely said,
   'Your Worship, please,

'I rise but briefly to agree
With what you said; for now I see
My client's guilty. But I pray
Your wonted mercy you this day
   Will show to him.

'I beg of you to set him free,
Scourge with your sharpest homily,
Yet, place him on a bond to keep
The public peace. How he doth weep!
   Oh, pity him!

'Poor boy! I know him college bred,
To learning he was nobly wed;
And it may glad your heart to know
He bore a rifle 'gainst the foe
    In glorious France!

'He comes of sires of that land
Beyond the Caspian, noble and . . .'
'What!' roared the Magistrate aloud
'Must I sit still while you becloud
My reason with your tommy-rot?
I swear by Justice I will not!
    Please, will you sit?'

The lawyer cried above the hum,
'When to this Court will Mercy come?
Time was—not long before you came—
She stooped to lend her sacred name
To that same Bench on which you sit,
And with her presence hallowed it,
    But now—alas! . . .'

His Worship purple in the face:
'How fallen thou from hope and grace,
O Ananias! Is it long
Since with that silver-coated tongue
You warbled thusly: "But I pray
Your wonted mercy you this day
    Will show to him?"

'Some day, no doubt, you will be made
A K.C.; yet, I am afraid,
Your eloquence will work you woe
In heaven above, or hell below,
    Or here between!

'One way my duty now doth lie!
I am of Spartan breed, and I
Will never hurt my conscience so
By letting such a culprit go
    Unpunished—free!

'For stealing of that duck, now, you
The prisoner, shall surely do
Six months' hard labour! That is that!
'Twere well, I think, to add "the cat"!
   There, take him down!'

Sam Droggan was to prison bound;
The lawyer he had earned his pound;
His worship hugged his Spartan pride;
And joyously, bill opened wide,
   'Quack!' said the duck.

ALFRED M. CRUICKSHANK
b Trinidad, 188?–194?

from *Poems in All Moods*, privately printed,
   Trinidad, 1937

REVOLT OF CHIEF TACKY

Tacky the chieftain decided to fight.
'I finish with being a slave.'
The morning sun rose clear and bright
On him and his followers brave,
   (His hundreds of followers brave).

So cunningly he laid his plan
So fierce his courage shone,
That up and down Jamaica land
Men made his cause their own,
   (They made his cause their own).

But one, faint-hearted, slipped away
Upon that fateful morn,
And many died on that sad day,
For soldiers had been warned,
   (Militia men were warned).

Oh sad it is to have to tell
But some the challenge spurned.
Once more, like slaves, their spirits fell;
To bondage they returned,
   (To bondage they returned).

But Coromantyne Tacky fought.
'As long as I have breath
No man shall boast that I was caught.'
A bullet caused his death,
   (Davy's bullet caused his death).

A bitter bullet laid him low.
No man knows where he lies.
So sing a mournful song and low
Beneath Jamaica skies,
   (For in this soil he lies).

ALMA NORMAN
b Canada, 1930

from *Ballads of Jamaica*, Longman, 1967

THE POND

There was this pond in the village
and little boys, he heard till he was sick,
were not allowed too near.
Unfathomable pool, they said,
that swallowed men and animals just so;
and in its depths, old people said,
swam galliwasps and nameless horrors;
bright boys kept away.

Though drawn so hard by prohibitions,
the small boy, fixed in fear, kept off;
till one wet summer, grass growing lush,
paths muddy, slippery, he found himself
there, at the fabled edge.

The brooding pond was dark.
Sudden, escaping cloud, the sun
came bright; and, shimmering in guilt,
he saw his own face peering from the pool.

MERVYN MORRIS
b Jamaica, 1937

THE VISIT

The keskidee calls stubbornly
From the lianas. A scramble of brambles
Tries the shut door.

Nobody in.
Perhaps there's been a gold rush,
Or something. This is a dead town.

But there's this clock,
Still ticking. And there's this stable
With the fresh smell of dung. Perhaps they'll be back

Soon.
So the stranger on horseback, in formal black,
Waited with an emissary's

Patience, while
The clock tocked and the stable dried,
The worms gained, and even the door

Fell in suddenly, on a clean, well-lighted
Place—

Then, as great birds came gliding in
Through the stretched jaws
Of the valley,

He was sure, and he turned,
Slapped leather twice
And rode off, his slowly cantering horse

Raising no echoes nor planting the least
Hoofprints in the indifferent clay . . .

WAYNE BROWN
b Trinidad, 1944

THE CASTLE

His mother told him of the king's
enormous thick-walled castle where
with lots of yellow courtiers
he kept his yellow court of fear.

The bold knight hopped a milk-white horse,
spurred fiercely, keen as anything;
resolved, this honourable knight,
to slay that fearful king.

The giddy knight rode hard and fast.
At dusk he heaved a dreadful sigh:
at last, that frightful yellow flag
against the darkening sky!

LIVING IS FEARING. Tired, he read
the writing on the castle wall,
and braced himself to slay that king
who terrifies us all.

The drawbridge down, the knight spurred hard,
galloping into battle;
but as he neared, the bridge pulled up
with a disdainful rattle.

Too late to stop, he took the plunge;
accoutred well, he couldn't float;
and, loud exclaiming 'Death to Fear!',
he drowned himself in the moat.

MERVYN MORRIS
b Jamaica, 1937

LE LOUPGAROU

A curious tale that threaded through the town
Through greying women sewing under eaves,
Was how his greed had brought old Le Brun down,
Greeted by slowly shutting jalousies
When he approached them in white-linen suit,
Pink glasses, cork hat, and tap-tapping cane,
A dying man licensed to sell sick fruit,
Ruined by fiends with whom he'd made a bargain.
It seems one night, these Christian witches said,
He changed himself to an Alsatian hound,
A slavering lycanthrope hot on a scent,
But his own watchman dealt the thing a wound
Which howled and lugged its entrails, trailing wet
With blood back to its doorstep, almost dead.

DEREK WALCOTT
b St Lucia, 1930

'Tales of the Islands, Chapter IX', from *In a Green Night*, Cape, 1962

THE TRUE GAGE

The room at first was merely a room,
Something to sleep in or work in,
Derive shelter from when it rained
Or the sky exploded at noon.

The room from that modest beginning
Proceeded to grow around him,
Or else it closed in while seeming
To extend on for miles in space.

The actual size of the room
Was, in fact, impressively normal,
But he never quite saw it right,
It was always too large or small.

One day, however, hearing the walls
Like temples about his ears,
He took a gun or a ruler,
Applied it, and got the true gage.

ANTHONY MCNEILL
b Jamaica, 1941

TO A CRIPPLED SCHOOLMASTER

We hogged the billiard table in your room,
We read your weekly *Mirrors* with delight,
Retailed your humorous pomposities
And roared with laughter at your sharp tongue's bite.

I still recall your dragging up the steps
And setting out some time before each bell;
I liked your funny classes (though in truth
I really cannot claim you taught us well).

Sadly we watched you grow from bad to worse,
Drag slower and slower until that summer term
You kept your room and classes came
To see you fade from ailing to infirm.

When you retired from teaching—as you had to,
When body couldn't serve your eager will—
We built a special house to cage you in
Where you could watch the football matches still.

Less often than I could I looked you up
And saw your living carcass wasting slow,
Your sprightliness of mind a crudish irony
When all your wretched limbs were withering so.

Without a conscious plan to be neglectful
I didn't seem to find the time
To drop in for your casual commentary
On what you called 'the national pantomime'.

I wonder whether time has stolen from me
Something that matters deeply (or should do)
And whether anything I manage now will ever
Quite kill my guilt about neglecting you.

And when you die I know I shall be sorry,
Remembering your kindness. But the fear
Of facing death stops me from coming
To see you dying smiling in your chair.

MERVYN MORRIS
b Jamaica, 1937
from *Commonwealth Poems of Today*, Murray, 1966

JAFFO THE CALYPSONIAN

Jaffo was a great calypsonian, a fire ate up his soul to sing and
    play calypso iron music.
Even when he was small he made many-coloured ping-pong
    drums and searched them for the island music,
Drums of beaten oil-barrel iron daubed in triangles with stolen
    paint from a harbour warehouse.
Now he seized the sorrow and the bawdy farce in metal-harsh
    beat and his own thick voice.
He was not famous in the tents: he went there once, and not a
    stone clapped, and he was afraid of respectable eyes:
The white-suited or gay-shirted lines of businessmen or tourists
    muffled his deep urge;
But he went back to the Indian tailor's shop and sang well, and
    to the Chinese sweet-and-sweepstake shop and sang well,
Unsponsored calypsoes; and in the scrap lots near the Dry River
    lit by one pitch-oil lamp or two
He would pound his ping-pong and sing his hoarse voice out
    for ragged still-eyed men.
But in the rum-shop he was best; drinking the heavy sweet
    molasses rum he was better than any other calypso man.
In front of the rows of dark red bottles, in the cane-scented
    rooms his clogged throat rang and rang with staccato shout.
Drunk, then, he was best; easier in pain from the cancer in his
    throat but holding the memory of it.
On the rough floors of rum-shops strewn with bottle-tops and
    silver-headed corks and broken green bottle-glass
He was released from pain into remembered pain, and his thick
    voice rose and grated in brassy fear and fierce joke,
His voice beat with bitterness and fun as if he told of old things,
    hurt ancestral pride, and great slave humour.
He would get a rum if he sang well, so perhaps there was that of
    it too.
He was always the best, though, he was the best: the ragged men
    said so and the old men.

One month before he died his voice thickened to a hard final
    silence.
The look of unsung calypsoes stared in his eyes, a terrible thing
    to watch in the rat-trap rum shops.

When he could not stand for pain he was taken to the public ward
of the Colonial Hospital.
Rafeeq, the Indian man who in Marine Square watches the birds
all day long for his God, was there also.
Later he told about Jaffo in a long mad chant to the rum-shop
men. They laughed at the story:
Until the end Jaffo stole spoons from the harried nurses to beat
out rhythm on his iron bedposts.

IAN MCDONALD
b Trinidad, 1933

from *Bim* 22, June 1955

Dialect into Poetry

A MARKET BASKET IN THE CAR

Why? doan't I pay me car-fare?
  Tuppence—same fe we two?
What you da mek up you face for?
  You tink I is frighten fe you?

Because you mudda see duppy,
  So put whitey wash in you 'kin,
Seems as you tink you is Buckra;
  You nigga man—ugly no sin.

Doan' dare you to come yah so push me,
  As in a' dis car I is sit;
I pay fe me fare an' I tell you
  De Gubbena self wouden' fit.

To come yah and f'erancing wid me,
  When I doan' brek none o' him rule;
Doan' liard, nor tief, nor obeah;
  An 'keep all me pickney a' school.

What you is saying?—O! 'nuttin''
  Dat is jus' what suiting you—Hi'
Keep grumblin' an' saying you 'nuttin'',
  While I drop you out a me eye.

TOM REDCAM
b Jamaica, 1870–1933

from *Orange Valley and Other Poems*, Pioneer Press, Jamaica, 1951

COLONISATION IN REVERSE

Wat a joyful news, Miss Mattie,
I feel like me heart gwine burs'
Jamaica people colonizin
Englan in reverse.

By de hundred, by de t'ousan
From country and from town,
By de ship-load, by de plane-load
Jamaica is Englan boun.

Dem a-pour out o' Jamaica,
Everybody future plan
Is fe get a big-time job
An settle in de mother lan.

What a islan! What a people!
Man an woman, old and young
Jusa pack dem bag an baggage
An tun history upside dung!

Some people don't like travel,
But fe show dem loyalty
Dem all a-open up cheap-fare-
To-Englan agency.

An week by week dem shippin off
Dem countryman like fire,
Fe immigrate an populate
De seat o' de Empire.

Oonoo see how life is funny,
Oonoo see de tunabout,
Jamaica live fe box bread
Outa English people mout'.

For wen dem catch a Englan,
An start play dem different role,
Some will settle down to work
An some will settle fe de dole.

Jane say de dole is not too bad
Bacause dey payin she
Two pounds a week fe seek a job
Dat suit her dignity.

Me say Jane will never find work
At the rate how she dah look,
For all day she stay pon Aunt Fan couch
An read love-story book.

Wat a devilment a Englan!
Dem face war an brave de worse,
But I'm wonderin how dem gwine stan
Colonizin in reverse.

LOUISE BENNETT
b Jamaica, 1919

from *Jamaica Labrish*, Sangster's Bookstores, Jamaica, 1966

from THE DUST

Yuh does get up, walk 'bout,
praise God that yuh body
int turnin' to stone,

an' that you bubbies still big;
that you got a good
voice that can shout

for heaven to hear
you: int got nothin' to fear
from no man. You does come

to the shop, stop, talk
little bit, get despatch
an' go home;

you still got a back that kin dig
in the fields
an' hoe an' pull up the weeds

from the peeny brown
square that you callin' your own;
you int sick an' you children strong;

ev'ry day you see the sun
rise, the sun
set; God sen' ev'ry month

a new moon. Dry season
follow wet season again
an' the green crop follow the rain.

An' then suddenly so
widdout rhyme
widdout reason

you crops start to die
you can't even see the sun in the sky;
an' suddenly so, without rhyme,

without reason, all you hope gone
ev'rything look like it comin' out wrong.
Why is that? What it mean?

EDWARD BRATHWAITE
b Barbados, 1930

from *Rights of Passage*, Oxford, 1967

UNCLE TIME

Uncle Time is a ole, ole man . . .
All year long 'im wash 'im foot in de sea
long, lazy years on de wet san'
an shake de coconut tree dem
quiet-like wid 'im sea-win laughter,
scraping away de lan' . . .

Uncle Time is a spider-man, cunnin' an cool,
him tell you: watch de hill an yu si me.
Huhh! Fe yu yi no quick enough fe si
how 'im move like mongoose; man, yu tink 'im fool?

Me Uncle Time smile black as sorrow;
'im voice is sof' as bamboo leaf
but Lawd, me Uncle cruel.
When 'im play in de street
wid yu woman,—watch 'im! By tomorrow
she dry as cane-fire, bitter as cassava;
an when 'im teach yu son, long after
yu walk wid stranger, an yu bread is grief.
Watch how 'im spin web roun yu house, an creep
inside; an when 'im touch yu, weep . . .

DENNIS SCOTT
b Jamaica, 1939

AN OLD JAMAICAN WOMAN THINKS ABOUT THE HEREAFTER

What would I do forever in a big place, who
have lived all my life in a small island?
The same parish holds the cottage I was born in, all
my family, and the cool churchyard.
                I have looked
up at the stars from my front verandah and have been afraid
of their pathless distances. I have never flown
in the loud aircraft nor have I seen palaces,
so I would prefer not to be taken up high nor
rewarded with a large mansion.
                I would like
to remain half-drowsing through an evening light
watching bamboo trees sway and ruffle for a valley-wind,
to remember old times but not to live them again;
occasionally to have a good meal with no milk
nor honey for I don't like them, and now and then to walk
by the grey sea-beach with two old dogs and watch
men bring up their boats from the water.
                For all this,
for my hope of heaven, I am willing to forgive my debtors
and to love my neighbour . . .
             although the wretch throws stones
at my white rooster and makes too much noise in her damn
                        backyard.

A. L. HENDRIKS
b Jamaica, 1922

from *On This Mountain*, Deutsch, 1965

Nature and Landscape: Trees

NOW THE LIGNUM VITAE BLOWS

Now the Lignum Vitae blows,
   Fair-browed April enters here,
In her hand a crimson rose,
   In her eye youth's crystal tear;
   Moonlit nights, serenely clear,
Rock the lilac-purpled bloom,
   Robes the Lignum Vitaes wear,
Fashioned at some mystic loom.

And the Brown Bee comes and goes,
   And his murmurous song I hear,
Like a dozing stream that flows
   To a drowsy, unseen mere,
   Deeply hid, but very near.
Rare the robes, the trees assume,
   Robes the Lignum Vitaes wear,
Fashioned at some mystic loom.

The grey Nightingale; he knows
   Music's mazes for the ear;
O'er the tinted petal snows,
   He, of Spring th' inspiréd Seer,
   Sings melodiously clear:
Rare as souls of soft perfume,
   Robes the Lignum Vitaes wear,
Fashioned at some mystic loom.

Envoi

All of April's fancy gear,
   None excels thee, fold or plume,
Flowers the Lignum Vitaes wear
   Fashioned at some mystic loom.

TOM REDCAM
b Jamaica, 1870–1933

from *Orange Valley and Other Poems*, Pioneer Press, Jamaica, 1951

THE CASTAWAYS

The vivid grass with visible delight
Springing triumphant from the pregnant earth,
The butterflies, and sparrows in brief flight
Dancing and chirping for the season's birth,
The dandelions and rare daffodils
That touch the deep-stirred heart with hands of gold,
The thrushes sending forth their joyous trills,—
Not these, not these did I at first behold!
But seated on the benches daubed with green,
The castaways of life, a few asleep,
Some withered women desolate and mean,
And over all, life's shadows dark and deep.
Moaning I turned away, for misery
I have the strength to bear but not to see.

CLAUDE MCKAY
b Jamaica, 1889–1944

from *Selected Poems of Claude McKay*, New York Bookman
     Associates Inc., 1953

IN A GREEN NIGHT

The orange tree, in various light,
Proclaims perfected fables now
That her last season's summer height
Bends from each over-burdened bough.

She has her winters and her spring,
Her moult of leaves, which in their fall
Reveal, as with each living thing,
Zones truer than the tropical.

For if by night each golden sun
Burns in a comfortable creed,
By noon harsh fires have begun
To quail those splendours which they feed.

Or mixtures of the dew and dust
That early shone her orbs of brass,
Mottle her splendours with the rust
She sought all summer to surpass.

By such strange, cyclic chemistry
That dooms and glories her at once
As green yet ageing orange tree,
The mind enspheres all circumstance.

No Florida loud with citron leaves
With crystal falls to heal this age
Shall calm the darkening fear that grieves
The loss of visionary rage.

Or if Time's fires seem to blight
The nature ripening into art,
Not the fierce noon or lampless night
Can quail the comprehending heart.

The orange tree, in various light
Proclaims that fable perfect now
That her last season's summer height
Bends from each over-burdened bough.

DEREK WALCOTT
b St Lucia, 1930
from *In a Green Night*, Cape, 1962

TELL ME TREES: WHAT ARE YOU WHISPERING?

It is strange
Standing here
Beneath the whispering trees
Far away from the haunts of men.
Tell me trees!
What are you whispering?

When I am dead
I shall come and lie
Beneath your fallen leaves . . .
But tell me trees,
What are you whispering?
They shall bury me
Beneath your fallen leaves.
My robe shall be
Green, fallen leaves,
My love shall be
Fresh fallen leaves.
My lips shall kiss
Sweet fallen leaves.
I and the leaves shall always lie together
And know no parting.

It is so strange
Standing here
Beneath the whispering trees!
Tell me, trees!
What are you whispering?

WILSON HARRIS
b Guyana, 1921

from *Themes of Song*, ed A. J. Seymour, Georgetown,
British Guyana, 1961

The Line of Literary Resistance

from DEATH OF A SLAVE

The cane field is green dark green
green with a life of its own.
The heart of a slave is red deep red
red with a life of its own.

Day passes like a long whip
over the back of a slave.
Day is a burning whip
Biting the neck of a slave.

But the sun falls down like an old man
beyond the dim line of the River,
and white birds
come flying, flying flapping at the wind
white birds like dreams come settling down.

Night comes from down river
like a thief–
Night comes from deep forest
in a boat of silence–
Dark is the shroud
the shroud of night
over the river
over the forest.

The slave staggers and falls
his face is on the earth
his drum is silent
silent like night
hollow like boat
between the tides of sorrow.
In the dark floor
In the cold dark earth
time plants the seeds of anger.

MARTIN CARTER
b Guyana, 1927

from *Poems of Resistance*, University of Guyana, 1964

THIS IS THE DARK TIME, MY LOVE

This is the dark time, my love.
All around the land brown beetles crawl about.
The shining sun is hidden in the sky.
Red flowers bend their heads in awful sorrow.

This is the dark time, my love.
It is the season of oppression, dark metal, and tears.
It is the festival of guns, the carnival of misery.
Everywhere the faces of men are strained and anxious.

Who comes walking in the dark night time?
Whose boot of steel tramps down the slender grass?
It is the man of death, my love, the stranger invader
watching you sleep and aiming at your dream.

MARTIN CARTER
b Guyana, 1927

from *Poems of Resistance*, University of Guyana, 1964

TILL I COLLECT

Over the shining mud the moon is blood
falling on ocean at the fence of lights.
My mast of love will sail and come to port
leaving a trail beneath the world, a track
cut by my rudder tempered out of anguish.

The fisherman will set his tray of hooks
and ease them one by one into the flood.
His net of twine will strain the liquid billow
and take the silver fishes from the deep.
But my own hand I dare not plunge too far
lest only sand and shells I bring to air
lest only bones I resurrect to light.

Over the shining mud the moon is blood
falling on ocean at the fence of lights—
My course I set, I give my sail the wind
to navigate the islands of the stars
till I collect my scattered skeleton
till I collect . . .

MARTIN CARTER
b Guyana, 1927

from *Poems of Resistance*, University of Guyana, 1964

THERE RUNS A DREAM

There runs a dream of perished Dutch plantations
In these Guiana rivers to the sea.
Black waters, rustling through the vegetation
That towers and tangles banks, run silently
Over lost stellings where the craft once rode
Easy before trim dwellings in the sun
And fields of indigo would float out broad
To lose the eye right on the horizon.

These rivers know that strong and quiet men
Drove back a jungle, gave Guiana root
Against the shock of circumstance, and then
History moved down river, leaving free
The forest to creep back, foot by quiet foot,
And overhang black waters to the sea.

A. J. SEYMOUR
b Guyana, 1914

from *Kyk-over-al*, Vol 6, No 19, Guyana, 1954

THIS LAND

Under this rhythm
Beats the voice
No one will notice.

Under this rock
Is the flame
No one sends freedom.

Under this island
Is the land
No one desires.

But in the time of drought
Is weeping
And in the time of harvest
Is weeping
And at the funeral
Is weeping
And in the marriage-bed
Is weeping.

Look O my Sun
Over this island
Look O my stars
Into this island.

For it sits upon the doorstep
And waits
And there is bleating in the dawn
And there is bleating in the night
For it sits upon the doorstep
And waits.

This land has no centre
Neither direction.
There is smoke without fire.
Life without movement.
   This! Oh my land.

M. G. SMITH
b Jamaica, 1921

SHEEP

God made sheep in the early morning.

In his hands he caught the clusters
Of the fleecy clouds of dawning
And tied them in bunches
And fastened their feet and their noses
With wet brown clay
And into their eyes he dropped
With reeds from a nearby river
The light of the dying morning star
And the light of the dying moon.

And then on that creation morning
When the sun had flooded the peaks and plains
And the dew lay thick on the rushes
Man saw sheep on the grazing grass
And heard the sadness of their bleating.

K. E. INGRAM
b Jamaica, 1921

from *A Treasury of Jamaican Poetry*,
University of London Press, 1949

Voices

THE CAT

Pleasures, that I most enviously sense,
   Pass in long ripples down her flanks and stir
   The plume that is her tail. She deigns to purr
And take caresses. But her paws would tense
To flashing weapons at the least offence.
   Humbly, I bend to stroke her silken fur,
   I am content to be a slave to her.
I am enchanted by her insolence.

No one of all the women I have known
   Has been so beautiful, or proud, or wise
   As this angora with her amber eyes.
She makes her chosen cushion seem a throne,
   And wears the same voluptuous, slow smile
   She wore when she was worshipped by the Nile.

W. ADOLPHE ROBERTS
b Jamaica, 1886–1962

from *A Treasury of Jamaican Poetry*,
University of London Press, 1949

from LEOPARD

Caught therefore in this care-
ful cage of glint, rock,

water ringing the islands'
doubt, his

terror dares
not blink. A nervous tick-

like itch picks
at the corners of his

lips. The lean flanks quick
and quiver until the

tension cracks his
ribs. If he could only

strike or trigger
off his fury. But cunning

cold bars break his
rage, and stretched to strike

his stretched claws strike
no glory.

EDWARD BRATHWAITE
b Barbados, 1930

from *Islands*, Oxford, 1969

A COMFORT OF CROWS

Mark this for a mercy: that here
birds, even here, sustain
the wide and impossible highways
of warm currents, divide the sky;
mark this—they all day have
amazed the air, that it falls apart
from their heavy wings in thin wedges
of sound; though the dull black earth
is very still, sweating
a special sourness
they make high over the hard thorn-trees
their own magnificence, turning,
they chain all together
with very slow journeys to and fro
the limits of the dead place,
smelling anything old and no longer quick.

Even here, though the rough ground
offers no kindness to the eye
nor the rusting engines could not ever
have intended an excellence of motion
and the stones have fallen in strange attitudes
and the boxes full of dry stained paper—
above the harsh barrows of land and metal
great birds pursue a vigilant silence.
The ceremonies of their soaring
have made a new and difficult solace:
there is no dead place nor dying so terrible
but weaves above it surely, breaking
the fragile air with beauty of its coming,
a comfort as of crows . . .

DENNIS SCOTT
b Jamaica, 1939

CARRION CROWS

Yes, I have seen them perched on paling posts—
Brooding with evil eyes upon the road,
Their black wings hooded—and they left these roosts

When I have hissed at them. Away they strode
Clapping their wings in a man's stride, away
Over the fields. And I have seen them feast
On swollen carrion in the broad eye of day,
Pestered by flies, and yet they never ceased.

But I have seen them emperors of the sky,
Balancing gracefully in the wind's drive
With their broad sails just shifting, or again
Throwing huge shadows from the sun's eye
To brush so swiftly over the field's plain,
And winnowing the air like beauty come alive.

A. J. SEYMOUR
b Guyana, 1914

from *Kyk-over-al*, Vol 6, No 19, 1954

PELICANS

In deserts of the bay
The Stylite pelicans
Watch the world pass away.

Each calmly meditates
Perched on a tarry baulk,
Immovable awaits

Answer to solemn prayer
Until a shoal of fish
Glitters in the dull air.

Then the rewarded saint
Is roused, and, taking wing,
With swerve and cunning feint

He stoops above the sea—
No shrill irreverend bird
Could show more cruelty.

EDWARD LUCIE-SMITH
b Jamaica, 1933

from *A Tropical Childhood and Other Poems*, Oxford, 1961

BIRD

That day the bird hunted an empty, gleaming sky
and climbed and coiled and spun measures of joy,
half-sleeping in the sly wind way
above my friend and me. Oh,
its wings' wind-flick and fleche were free
and easy in the sun, and a whip's tip
tracing of pleasure its mute madrigal,
that I below watched it so tall
it could not fall save slow
down the slow day.

'What is it?' said my friend.
'Yonder . . . .'
                  Hill and home patterned and curved
and frozen in the white round air
'Yes, there,' he said, 'I see it—'
                      Up
the steep sky till the eye
lidded from weight of sun on earth and wing!

'Watch this,' he said, bending for stones,
and my boy's throat grew tight with warning
to the bird that rode the feathered morning.

'Now there's a good shot, boy!' he said.
I was only ten then.
'If you see any more be sure to shout
but don't look at the sun too long,' he said,
'makes your eyes run.'

DENNIS SCOTT
b Jamaica, 1939

from *Young Commonwealth Poets '65*, Heinemann, 1966

MACKEREL

Deeper, running
deeper, dropping away,
slipping the clutch of our cold sun
swam the driven shoal—all but one
who stayed, turning mildly
about the same calm plaque of sea
on a casual quest, forgetting time.

From the shelf of a rank, barnacled rock
I watched him: vague-tailed, indifferent, almost a drifting crease of blue,
he seemed for a time at ease: secure
with his secret and indolent with knowledge
and all given over to the surge of the sea. Then

Lost, in a quick panic,
beating left and right, an addict
scouring his place for some misplaced fix, spun by the under
waves of time.

Finally, steadied as by a new
purpose, he sank, fin-thrilling.
His curled, blue back
shone in a crackle of sunlight
and was gone,

And I, staring, peering from my shelf
with the curiosity of a child and a child's
horror, knew he would not return,
though the wild, cheated gulls
still churned overhead, screaming.

2

The green crystal of our nether world
yielded nothing now; yet
men will have their truths,
their tidy legends, their
ends; so I

Imagine him, risen elsewhere,
thrown ashore where the white wave spills
and ageing, his round glass eye dulled;
or crammed to the gills
in the craw of a shark; or thrashing, culled
on the end of a line;

And only deny
that somewhere, hanging in streams
of light, some ice-blue Purpose
keeps in quiet its
unfathomable self,
given over, all
over, with easy fins,
to the timeless surge of the sea.

WAYNE BROWN
b Trinidad, 1944

HIGH NOON

At twelve o'clock the maddened sun charges
the city; a flourish of klaxons, cycle bells,
and counter-clerks hurrying to their
appointed meal prelude his daily tantrum.

Watch him propel his entrance from a door
sprung vertical to the reflector-sky—
a frothing bull dropped into the arena
of guttered streets and wilted wooden houses.

His purpled rage disintegrates the asphalt,
and city folk, entrenched in sheltered niches,
helplessly view the wanton holocaust
of brittle grass, and paint-peeled walls, and trees
stoutly assuaging heat for park-benched stragglers.

Blindly he flings his fury at closed doors
of shops, and errant drays wheel cautiously
along the vacant streets once thick with noise.
His frenzy spent, he squats above the square
surveying in disdain the rampage grounds . . .

And people stir and the bustling city throws
taunts of indifference at this jaded foe
as chatter surges and the cycle bells
resume their spate of talk at one o'clock.

RAYMOND BARROW
b British Honduras, 1920

from *Caribbean Quarterly*, Vol 5, No 3, 1958

THE HURRICANE
after Hokusai

Come where on this last shore of broken teeth
All spume and fury of snorting battle-horses,
Wild waves and trees are lashing their drenched hair
Like treacherous women come to grief,
In grey, uproarious war, charge after charge
Of hurtling cavalry shuddering the shore,
Deafening the birdless marge!
Find the storm's swirling core, and understand
That mad, old fisherman dancing on his barge,
Yelling and poling as it wheels around
Its hollow boasts of cataclysmic sound.

Study the grey storm streak his hair, and prize
More than those hoarse cauldrons heaven has upended
The salt delight of wrinkled eyes,
And his strange sorrow when all storms are ended.

DEREK WALCOTT
b St Lucia, 1930

from *In a Green Night*, Cape, 1962

DROUGHT

The woman is barren. And the blackbirds
have had a hard time this year with the drought
and fallen like moths to the field's floor.

The woman is barren. And the city,
crawling south like an oil-slick
will soon be around her ankles.

So she sings: 'Will you marry me?
I will go searching under many flat stones
for moisture of the departed rains.'

Sings: O world, will you marry me?

The riverbed's dried up completely, the lizards
have taken to the trees, to the high branches.
The cane rolls westwards, burning burning

In the sunset of her time, in the ploughed crater
where the woman like a frail apostrophe
dances palely each evening

Among the fallen blackbirds.

WAYNE BROWN
b Trinidad, 1944

SOUL ON ICE

Instantly the horizon tilts and whirls
to a white sky, emptied of geese.
Listen. It seems

Years since the ant-trek team
of huskies scrawled across this snow
leaving no trail, leaving

Me, the landscape, shimmering, waiting for words.
The syntax of solitude is thickening
my tongue. I cannot bend my back.

What noise is that, the river's roar,
or the city's avalanche of words
crashing and breaking far away?

Shall I be a child, shall I
die alone, away from the dogs' hot
breath? I can decipher nothing now.

The sun's effort
glows and fades. White napkins
are floating down. Shall I

Startle the fossils while yet I think
of trees, white-thighed, whipping about
for our lost love, yours too?

This is our pale vaudeville
so let us dance: the ape's skeleton, erect,
and the ghost. Characters of the

Apocalypse! I am bored
with stares, what I want now
are all those truths the prophets told,

Memory, infancy, where it went wrong,
the ice-flash,
the mastodon, the mastodon!

Listen
It seems years . . .

WAYNE BROWN
b Trinidad, 1944

HISTORY LESSON

Poised on his dusty pedagogic dais,
'Your history prep,' he said 'is a disgrace' . . .
But no surprise showed in a face.

'So, after class, you'll all stay in to con
'That chapter of our set book—Meiklejohn
'On the British Constitution'.

'But, *please*, sir' Cromwell junior starts to fuss,
'What's British history's got to do with *us*?'
(Some murmur of a *sotto voce* cuss . . .)

'You'll soon find out, you cheeky young baboon . . .
'Just fail your School Certificate next June,
'Then you'll pipe another tune!'

(Ten-sixty-six to fourteen-eighty-five . . .
For me the period dates alone survive
Of all that immemorial jive.)

Where are they now, who formed that College class?
. . . *Mirabile dictu* . . . so it came to pass
That Cromwell failed, and left at Michaelmas,

Who now, a diplomat, at fifty-three,
Has 'made it' . . . with a (Civ. Div.) O.B.E.,
Or, as they say, 'made history'.

VIVIAN VIRTUE
b Jamaica, 1911

THE LESSON

'Your father's gone,' my bald headmaster said.
His shiny dome and brown tobacco jar
Splintered at once in tears. It wasn't grief.
I cried for knowledge which was bitterer
Than any grief. For there and then I knew
That grief has uses—that a father dead
Could bind the bully's fist a week or two;
And then I cried for shame, then for relief.

I was a month past ten when I learnt this:
I still remember how the noise was stilled
In school-assembly when my grief came in.
Some goldfish in a bowl quietly sculled
Around their shining prison on its shelf.
They were indifferent. All the other eyes
Were turned towards me. Somewhere in myself
Pride, like a goldfish, flashed a sudden fin.

EDWARD LUCIE-SMITH
b Jamaica, 1933

from *A Tropical Childhood and Other Poems*,
    Oxford, 1961

THE DUMB-SCHOOL TEACHER

He made them books,
turning the leaves
of his hands
like old, cracked testaments;
between the lines
they read his love.
Words had shapes
changeable as
aspects of the truth
they learned,
talking of grief and glory
with the same quick palms.
And what a gossip in the eye,
what a babble
of necessary, sleight-
of-hand!

      So when he died
they spoke of his folded
lips in whispers,
making no distinction
between prayers at his passing
and their talk of weather
and wonder. He most of men
they knew
found endless praise
in the silence of their chatter,
their moving hands
his
monument.

DENNIS SCOTT
b Jamaica, 1939

A LESSON FOR THIS SUNDAY

The growing idleness of summer grass
With its frail kites of furious butterflies
Requests the lemonade of simple praise
In scansion gentler than my hammock swings
And rituals no more upsetting than a
Black maid shaking linen as she sings
The plain notes of some protestant hosanna
Since I lie idling from the thought in things,

Or so they should. Until I hear the cries
Of the small children hunting yellow wings,
Who break my sabbath with the thought of sin.
Brother and sister, with a common pin,
Frowning like serious lepidopterists.
The little surgeon pierces the thin eyes.
Crouched on plump haunches, as a mantis prays
She shrieks to eviscerate its abdomen.
The lesson is the same. The maid removes
Both prodigies from their interest in science.
The girl, in lemon frock, begins to scream
As the maimed, teetering thing attempts its flight.
She is herself a thing of summery light,
Frail as a flower in this blue August air,
Not marked for some late grief that cannot speak.

The mind swings inward on itself in fear
Swayed towards nausea from each normal sign.
Heredity of cruelty everywhere,
And everywhere the frocks of summer torn,
The long look back to see where choice is born,
As summer grass sways to the scythe's design.

DEREK WALCOTT
b St Lucia, 1930

from *In a Green Night*, Cape, 1962

FOR PALINURUS, THE LOST HELMSMAN

Too much you trusted the calm of the sea and the skies
Too much, Palinurus, you trusted.
We were hugging dreams of how sweetly
The waves were crooning against our bows—
Your splash into water joined the voices
That secured our dreams.
Too much you trusted, helmsman; your passengers
Slept too well.

Now naked, unknown, unknowing the sea,
Your body will drift to the beach;
To some beach, somewhere, calm, yellow and unknown.

JOHN FIGUEROA
b Jamaica, 1920

from *Love Leaps Here*, 1962

NOAH

Everywhere fish wheeled and fled,
Or died in scores, floating like eggs,
From his mind's ark. Noah,
Sailor for the kingdom of Truth's sake,
Watched the waters close like mouths
Over the last known hills. Next day
He slept, dreaming of haystacks.

Water woke him. He stood, arms folded,
Looking from a porthole, thinking nothing,
Numbed to a stare by horizon's drone, and the
Dry patter of rain. On the third day,
Decisive, sudden, he dragged
Down the canvas curtains and turned
Inward to tend his animals, his
Animals, waking with novelty.

Locked, driven by fatigue, the ark
Beat and beat across the same sea,
Bloated, adrift, finding
Nothing to fasten to.
Barnacles grew up the sides like sores. Inside,

Noah, claustrophobic, sat and watched
The occupants of his ark take on
New aspects, shudder into focus, one
By one. Something, he thought, must come
Of this. Such isolation! Such concentration!
Out of these instinctual, half-lit lives,
Something; some good, some Truth!
That night a dropped calf bawled to its feet,
Shaking off light like dirt.

Noah, an old man, unhappy shook
His head. Birth was not the answer,
Nor death: his mind's ark stank
Of death and birth, would always,
Sundering, stink. Outside,
The hard, insistent patter of rain
Saying 'Think, Noah, think! Break this

Patter of rain, man!' But only animals
Moved in his mind. Now, unbodied by raindrops,
The patter continued, empty, shelled,
Clambering down along itself, like crabs.
Driven, impotent, he neared despair. Finally,
One bird, unasked, detached itself
And battered around inside his skull.

Thankfully Noah released it, fearful,
Hoping, watching it flit and bang
Against wind, returning each time
Barren. One day, laden with lies,
It brought back promise of fruit,
Of resolution and change.

Now animals and men crowded the gangplank
Peering eagerly about the returning hills for
Some sign of change. Noah conducted them,
Drifting among valleys with breaking smiles
Naming, explaining, directing; Noah, relieved,
Turned once more outwards, giving thanks.

Relief dazed him: nobody realised
Nothing had changed. Elephant and insect
Settled quickly to old moulds, un-
Remembered seasons of death and birth,
Led by the bearded one, the prophet, Noah

Rejuvenated, giving thanks on a hill,
Moving among known animals and men
With a new aspect, giving thanks . . .
While leaking derelict, its mission abandoned,
The ark of his mind
Wallowed, empty, westward
To where all rainbows
Drown among waves.

WAYNE BROWN
b Trinidad, 1944

from *Jamaica Journal*, Vol 3, No 3, 1969

COLUMBUS

To find the Western path,
Right thro' the Gates of Wrath . . .

BLAKE

As I walked with my friend,
My singular Columbus,
Where the land comes to an end
And the path is perilous,
Where the wheel and tattered shoe
And bottle have been thrown,
And the sky is shining blue,
And the heart sinks like a stone,

I plucked his sleeve and said,
'I have come far to find
The springs of a broken bed,
The ocean, and the wind.
I'd rather live in Greece,
Castile, or an English town
Than wander here like this
Where the dunes come tumbling down.'

He answered me, 'Perhaps.
But Europe never guessed
America, their maps
Could not describe the West.
And though in Plato's glass
The stars were still and clear,
Yet nothing came to pass
And men died of despair.'

He said, 'If there is not
A way to China, one
City surpassing thought,
My ghost will still go on.
I'll spread the airy sail,'
He said, 'and point the sprit
To a country that cannot fail,
For there's no finding it.'

Straightway we separated—
He, in his fading coat,
To the water's edge, where waited
An admiral's longboat.
A crew of able seamen
Sprang up at his command—
An angel or a demon—
And they rowed him from the land.

LOUIS SIMPSON
b Jamaica, 1923

from *Selected Poems*, Oxford, 1966

DEATH OF A COMRADE

Death must not find us thinking that we die.

Too soon, too soon
our banner draped for you.
I would prefer
the banner in the wind
not bound so tightly
in a scarlet fold—
not sodden sodden
with your people's tears
but flashing on the pole
we bear aloft
down and beyond this dark dark lane of rags.

Dear Comrade
if it must be
you speak no more with me
nor smile no more with me
then let me take
a patience and a calm—
for even now the greener leaf explodes
sun brightens stone
and all the river burns.

Now from the mourning vanguard moving on
dear Comrade I salute you and I say
Death will not find us thinking that we die.

MARTIN CARTER
b Guyana, 1927

from *Poems of Resistance*, University of Guyana, 1964

CORTÈGE

Their grief's wind blows him
three and a half miles home
to freedom, their black hands
limp, lowered like flags
feet stuttering
an alphabet of faith,

for his armour is
finally bronze, his weapon
silence and that green farm wagon
thousands attend, his chariot.

           This last
march is the loneliest.
           Yet
concealed, in the slow mules'
clatter, the mourners' feet
measuring loss
by the long Atlanta street

he shares a dream
that hope
in this funeral harvest of lilies will
let freedom ring,
the wounding, sworded South
healed in some ploughshare Spring.

DENNIS SCOTT
b Jamaica, 1939

DON

for the D
'To John Coltrane: the heaviest spirit'
from *Black Music*, LeRoi Jones

may I learn the shape of that hurt
which captured you nightly into
dread city, discovering through
streets steep with the sufferer's beat:

teach me to walk through jukeboxes
and shadow that broken music
whose irradiant stop is light,
guide through those mournfullest journeys

I back into harbour Spirit
in heavens remember we now
and show we a way into praise,
all seekers together, one-heart:

and let we lock conscious when wrong
and Babylon rock back again:
in the evil season sustain
o heaviest spirit of sound.

ANTHONY MCNEILL
b Jamaica, 1941

67

from NEW WORLD A-COMIN'

It will be a long long time before we see
this land again, these trees
again, drifting inland with the sound
of surf, smoke rising

It will be a long long time before we see
these farms again, soft wet slow green
again: Aburi, Akwamu,
mist rising

Watch now these hard men, cold
clear eye'd like the water we ride,
skilful with sail and the rope and the tackle

Watch now these cold men, bold
as the water banging the bow in a sudden wild tide,
indifferent, it seems, to the battle

of wind in the water;
for our blood, mixed
soon with their passion in sport,

in indifference, in anger,
will create new soils, new souls, new
ancestors; will flow like this tide fixed

to the star by which this ship floats
to new worlds, new waters, new
harbours, the pride of our ancestors mixed

with the wind and the water
the flesh and the flies, the whips and the fixed
fear of pain in this chained and welcoming port.

EDWARD BRATHWAITE
b Barbados, 1930

from *Rights of Passage*, Oxford, 1967

So, goodbye to dark:
these black clowns and their manacled capers,
that brooding of hills. We sail
at dusk, taking the tide out
by the moon's chronometer.
The island floats behind
me not leaving,
dragging itself in the ship's road by
a seaweed cord.
The deck smells
of sugar and spices, spiders breed
their scuttling memories in
the green banana stems
below, the Captain tells me;
and below, I am glad to be gone.

Yet the hills are woodcut wild,
inked at my heart
and hard to erase;
to the last I possess them,
their branches, their sun,
the carved black dancers—
I have printed myself
their wooden glances
with an iron pride
more savage than theirs.
I have signed them.

The paper darkens
away from that porthole moon,
a fistful of wind
bellies us North North East;
turn in.

The spiders
throw their silk across the hold,
and turning fruit prepare
a tropic gold. Perhaps
when London snows
I shall be sad
buying their sweet
splendour, to recall
the green remaining.
Sea knots slip
apart; only the past permits
no unchaining.

DENNIS SCOTT
b Jamaica, 1939

from *Jamaica Journal*, Vol 3, No 3, 1969

KITE-FLYING
Kensington Gardens, London

It's a long time since
I last flew, or even saw one flown,
In my skylarking days . . .
Since my bamboo kite leaped on the breeze,
Climbing the sky unsteadily, swishing
Its tail, straining the leash,
Whining like a hound beyond the trees,
Dizzy above the village,—
Then breaking loose with a snap,
Disappearing, entangled in some treetop
  Inaccessible backyards away.

Then there were duels,
When our rival kites rose menacing,
Armed with glinting pieces of glass,
Or rusty razor blades—parrying, hissing,
Rushing, dodging expertly, up and down . . .
No two cocks more gamely
Spurred and pecked at each other,
Until, inevitably,
One was sliced, cut down reeling,
Blown so bravely
  Out of sight!

I've come a long way
To capture again, unexpectedly,
For a many-coloured, singing moment,
The fugitive kite that escaped
  Beyond my boyhood.

VIVIAN VIRTUE
b Jamaica, 1911

THE ROOM

The room
in which they've hung
the halfmillion Cezanne
is silent
the atmosphere wan
like in church
worshippers
pressed against a far wall
afraid of committing sacrilege
intent
on the delicate intellectual colouring
parody of a lunch on the grass
bad drawing
the oldmasters privilege
One young woman has a hunch
the State has been swindled
braves the awed silence
approaches the canvas
lit like a billboard
trying to see the money

CLIFF LASHLEY
b Jamaica, 1935

THE HARLEM DANCER

Applauding youths laughed with young prostitutes
And watched her perfect, half-clothed body sway;
Her voice was like the sound of blended flutes
Blown by black players upon a picnic day.
She sang and danced on gracefully and calm,
The light gauze hanging loose about her form;
To me she seemed a proudly-swaying palm,
Grown lovelier for passing through a storm.
Upon her swarthy neck black shiny curls
Luxuriant fell; and tossing coins in praise,
The wine-flushed, bold-eyed boys, and even the girls,
Devoured her shape with eager, passionate gaze;
But looking at her falsely-smiling face,
I knew her self was not in that strange place.

CLAUDE MCKAY
b Jamaica, 1899–1944

from *Selected Poems of Claude McKay*, New York Bookman
    Associates Inc., 1953

I SHALL RETURN

I shall return again, I shall return
To laugh and love and watch with wonder-eyes
At golden noon the forest fires burn,
Wafting their blue-black smoke to sapphire skies.
I shall return to loiter by the streams
That bathe the brown blades of the bending grasses,
And realize once more my thousand dreams
Of waters surging down the mountain passes.
I shall return to hear the fiddle and fife
Of village dances, dear delicious tunes
That stir the hidden depths of native life,
Stray melodies of dim-remembered runes.
I shall return. I shall return again
To ease my mind of long, long years of pain.

CLAUDE MCKAY
b Jamaica, 1889–1944

from *Selected Poems of Claude McKay*, New York Bookman
Associates Inc., 1953

SOUTH

But today I recapture the islands'
bright beaches: blue mist from the ocean
rolling into the fishermen's houses.
By these shores I was born: sound of the sea
came in at my window, life heaved and breathed in me then
with the strength of that turbulent soil.

Since then I have travelled: moved far from the beaches:
sojourned in stoniest cities, walking the lands of the north
in sharp slanting sleet and the hail,
crossed countless saltless savannas and come
to this house in the forest where the shadows oppress me
and the only water is rain and the tepid taste of the river.

We who are born of the ocean can never seek solace
in rivers: their flowing runs on like our longing,
reproves us our lack of endeavour and purpose,
proves that our striving will founder on that.
We resent them this wisdom, this freedom: passing us
toiling, waiting and watching their cunning declension down to
    the sea.

But today I would join you, travelling river,
borne down the years of your patientest flowing,
past pains that would wreck us, sorrows arrest us,
hatred that washes us up on the flats;
and moving on through the plains that receive us,
processioned in tumult, come to the sea.

Bright waves splash up from the rocks to refresh us,
blue sea-shells shift in their wake
and *there* is the thatch of the fishermen's houses, the path
made of pebbles, and look!
Small urchins combing the beaches
look up from their traps to salute us:

they remember us just as we left them.
The fisherman, hawking the surf on this side
of the reef, stands up in his boat
and halloos us: a starfish lies in its pool.
And gulls, white sails slanted seaward,
fly into the limitless morning before us.

EDWARD BRATHWAITE
b Barbados, 1930

from *Rights of Passage*, Oxford, 1967

SQUATTER'S RITES

Peas, corn, potatoes; he had
planted himself
king of a drowsy hill; no one
cared how he came to such green dignity,
scratching his majesty
among the placid chickens.

But after a time, after
his deposition, the uncivil wind
snarled anarchy through that
small kingdom. Trees, wild birds
troubled the window,
as though to replace the fowl
that wandered and died of summer;
spiders locked the door,
threading the shuddered moths,
and stabbed their twilight needles through
that grey republic. The parliament of dreams
dissolved. The shadows tilted
where leaf-white, senatorial lizards
inhabited his chair.

Though one of his sons made it,
blowing reggae (he
dug city life)
enough to bury the old Ras
with respect
ability and finally,
a hole in his heart;

and at night when the band
played soul, the trumpet
pulse beat
down the hill
to the last post,
abandoned,

leaning in its hole
like a sceptre
among the peas, corn, potatoes.

DENNIS SCOTT
b Jamaica, 1939   77

ANCESTORS

Every Friday morning my grandfather
left his farm of canefields, chickens, cows,
and rattled in his trap down to the harbour town
to sell his meat. He was a butcher.
Six-foot-three and very neat: high collar,
winged, a grey cravat, a waistcoat, watch-
chain just above the belt, thin narrow-
bottomed trousers, and the shoes his wife
would polish every night. He drove the trap
himself: slap of the leather reins
along the horse's back and he'd be off
with a top-hearted homburg on his head:
black English country gentleman.

Now he is dead. The meat shop burned,
his property divided. A doctor bought
the horse. His mad alsatians killed it.
The wooden trap was chipped and chopped
by friends and neighbours and used to stop-
gap fences and for firewood. One yellow
wheel was rolled across the former cowpen gate.
Only his hat is left. I 'borrowed' it.
I used to try it on and hear the night wind
man go battering through the canes, cocks waking up and thinking
it was dawn throughout the clinking country night.
Great caterpillar tractors clatter down
the broken highway now; a diesel engine grunts
where pigs once hunted garbage.
A thin asthmatic cow shares the untrashed garage.

2
All that I can remember of his wife,
my father's mother, is that she sang us songs
('Great Tom Is Cast' was one), that frightened me.
And she would go chug-chugging with a jar
of milk until its white pap turned to yellow
butter. And in the basket underneath the stairs
she kept the polish for grandfather's shoes.

All that I have of her is voices:
laughing me out of fear because a crappaud
jumped and splashed the dark where I was huddled
in the galvanized tin bath; telling us stories
round her fat white lamp. It was her Queen
Victoria lamp, she said; although the stamp
read Ever Ready. And in the night, I listened to her singing
in a Vicks and Vapour Rub-like voice what you would call the
    blues

3
Come-a look
come-a look
see wha' happen

come-a look
come-a look
see wha' happen

Sookey dead
Sookey dead
Sookey dead-o

Sookey dead
Sookey dead
Sookey dead-o.

Him a-wuk
him a-wuk
till 'e bleed-o

him a-wuk
him a-wuk
till 'e bleed-o

Sookey dead
Sookey dead
Sookey dead-o

Sookey dead
Sookey dead
Sookey dead-o . . .

EDWARD BRATHWAITE
b Barbados, 1930

from *Islands*, Oxford, 1969

WHO'S SAMMY?

The white face of Sammy, that mad
clown. I can't sleep,
He's dancing amid the sheets. Can
see him again, elusive, pale,
pushing dope and some fairy tale.

Who's Sammy? Sammy's a mad.
Who's Sammy? Sammy's a clock.
In the dark, Sammy goes tick tock.
Sammy's a sock

Wham! in the brain.
But most of all, Sammy's a mad,
Sammy's a strange.
I say: flush Sammy down the drain,
He's a dancing blot on my brain.

Midnight. Sammy's still loud.
Sammy's a clod.
When he fell, his white face splintered and bled.
Several weeks dead,
He's a dancing duppy above my bed.

Who's Sammy? Sammy's a demon.
Sammy's a child's fairy garden.
A sinister leer.
The perfect March Hare.

But suppose Sammy's some more,
Suppose he's a wound apart from a stain,
'A subtle buffoon and Jesus-man,
who, pinned to a lewd grin,
undertakes for us all
the clown's crucifixion'?

ANTHONY MCNEILL
b Jamaica, 1941

OGUN

My uncle made chairs, tables, balanced doors on, dug out
coffins, smoothing the white wood out

with plane and quick sandpaper until
it shone like his short-sighted glasses.

The knuckles of his hands were sil-
vered knobs of nails hit, hurt and flat-

tened out with blast of heavy hammer. He was knock-knee'd, flat-
footed and his clip clop sandals slapped across the concrete

flooring of his little shop where canefield mulemen and a fleet
of Bedford lorry drivers dropped in to scratch themselves and talk.

There was no shock of wood, no beam
of light mahogany his saw teeth couldn't handle.

When shaping squares for locks, a key hole
care tapped rat tat tat upon the handle

of his humpbacked chisel. Cold
world of wood caught fire as he whittled: rectangle

window frames, the intersecting x of fold-
ing chairs, triangle

trellises, the donkey
box-cart in its squeaking square.

But he was poor and most days he was hungry.
Imported cabinets with mirrors, formica table

tops, spine-curving chairs made up of tubes, with hollow
steel-like bird bones that sat on rubber ploughs,

thin beds, stretched not on boards, but blue high-tensioned
    cables,
were what the world preferred.

And yet he had a block of wood that would have baffled them.
With knife and gimlet care he worked away at this on Sundays,

explored its knotted hurts, cutting his way
along its yellow whorls until his hands could feel

how it had swelled and shivered, breathing air,
its weathered green burning to rings of time,

its contoured grain still tuned to roots and water.
And as he cut, he heard the creak of forests:

green lizard faces gulped, grey memories with moth
eyes watched him from their shadows, soft

liquid tendrils leaked among the flowers
and a black rigid thunder he had never heard within his hammer

came stomping up the trunks. And as he worked within his
    shattered
Sunday shop, the wood took shape: dry shuttered

eyes, slack anciently everted lips, flat
ruined face, eaten by pox, ravaged by rat

and woodworm, dry cistern mouth, cracked
gullet crying for the desert, the heavy black

enduring jaw; lost pain, lost iron;
emerging woodwork image of his anger.

EDWARD BRATHWAITE
b Barbados, 1930

from *Islands*, Oxford, 1969

ALLEGRE

Some mornings are as full of elation
As these pigeons crossing the hill slopes,
Silver as they veer in sunlight and white
On the warm blue shadows of the range.

And the sunward sides of the shacks
Gilded, as though this was Italy.

The bird's claws fasten round the lignum-vitae,
The roots of delight growing downward,
As the singer in his prime.

And the slopes of the forest this sunrise
Are thick with blue haze, as the colour
Of the woodsmoke from the first workman's fire.
A morning for wild bees and briersmoke,
For hands cupped to boys' mouths, the holloa
Of their cries in the cup of the valley.

The stream keeps its edges, wind-honed,
As the intellect is clear in affections,
Calm, with the rivulet's diligence.

Men are sawing with the wind on those ridges,
Trees arching, campeche, gommiers, canoe-wood,
The sawn trunks trundled down hillsides
To crash to the edge of the sea.
No temples, yet the fruits of intelligence,
No roots, yet the flowers of identity,
No cities, but white seas in sunlight,
Laughter and doves, like young Italy.

Yet to find the true self is still arduous,
And for us, especially, the elation can be useless and empty
As this pale, blue ewer of the sky,
Loveliest in drought.

DEREK WALCOTT
b St Lucia, 1930

from *In a Green Night*, Cape, 1962

THE KNIFE OF DAWN

I make my dance right here!
Right here on the wall of prison I dance.
This world's hope is a blade of fury
and we who are sweepers of an ancient sky
discoverers of new planets, sudden stars
we are the world's hope.
And so therefore I rise again I rise again
freedom is a white road with green grass like love.

Out of my time I carve a monument
out of a jagged block of convict years I carve it.
The sharp knife of dawn glitters in my hand
but how bare is everything—tall tall tree
infinite air, the unrelaxing tension of the world
and only hope, hope only, the kind eagle soars and
    wheels in flight.

I dance on the wall of prison
it is not easy to be free and bold
it is not easy to be poised and bound
it is not easy to endure the spike—
so river flood, drench not my pillar feet
so river flood, collapse to estuary
only the heart's life, the kind eagle, soars and
    wheels in flight.

MARTIN CARTER
b Guyana, 1927

from *Poems of Resistance*, University of Guyana, 1964

84

Commentary
and
Questions for Discussion in Class

Making

The poems in this group have to do with the act of making something, and so lend themselves to being studied together—if only as a way of bringing out the special qualities of each.

They are also illustrative of three distinct phases in West Indian poetry. Early West Indian poetry too often ignored the common sights and sounds around and too often had the static feel of the verandah or the middle-class drawing room. Virtue's *Landscape Painter*, written in the 1960's, is an outdoor poem, and it does not have the more obvious stylistic weaknesses of early poems such as *Now the Lignum Vitae Blows* or *Henry's Ambition*. But the carefully composed scene, although taking place out of doors, gives the impression more of indoor activity transferred to a sheltered outside than of a participation in the life of nature or of a community. Virtue's poem indeed is a continuation of an early kind to which *Road-mending* reads like a deliberate reaction. Ramon-Fortuné's poem, written in the early 1950's, finds its inspiration in an ordinary, seemingly un-poetic activity. In the phase of which *Road-mending* is an example, West Indian poets find matter for their poems everywhere among the lives of the people and in the landscape in which they are seen as moving. This phase also includes social realism and a protest tendency which are very marked in West Indian prose of the 1930's and 1940's.

In the 1960's we begin to see the emergence of West Indian poets such as Derek Walcott, Edward Brathwaite, Dennis Scott, Tony McNeill, Mervyn Morris and Wayne Brown, each with his own voice or voices, each with his own way of seeing, and each confident enough in his craft and in his own vision to follow the poem wherever it leads. As this collection illustrates, the poets use a variety of styles and cover a wide range of material. In *Discoverer*, Edward Brathwaite moves backward in time, allowing the imagination to dwell upon a crucial moment in Caribbean history when the discoverer is disconcerted by the new land upon which he has dreamily burst. The poem seems to imply that if the relationship between invader and invaded had been directly influenced by such moments of self-discovery and humility as Columbus's at this point, the history of the Caribbean might not have been so full of brutality and exploitation.

LANDSCAPE PAINTER, JAMAICA (p 2)

[a] Who is the watcher (the 'I') in this poem? Who is being watched?

[b] What impression does line 6 create? What features, in addition to the actual meaning of the words, help to create this impression?

[c] Mime the action of the fourth stanza to show you understand it.

[d] Why do you think the poet uses the word 'fidgeting' about the hills?

[e] What feeling is the poet trying to communicate? How do you know?

[f] Why is the watcher so interested in the watched?

ROAD-MENDING (p 3)

[a] Who is the speaker in this poem? Does he enter the poem in the way the poet does in *Landscape Painter, Jamaica*? What marks the difference between the two poems in this respect?

[b] What is the poet suggesting that the road-mender's activity is like?

[c] Look at the arrangement of the lines in the first stanza. In what way does it support the sense of the stanza? Would you also say that the line arrangement in stanza two supports the sense of the stanza?

[d] Is the rhythm of *Road-Mending* more marked than that in *Landscape Painter, Jamaica*? If so, what makes it so? Bearing in mind the different activities involved, would you say that the rhythm is appropriate in each of these poems?

DISCOVERER (p 4)

[a] Who is the sailor in this poem? What do you know about him?

[b] Who is the poet pretending to be in the first five stanzas? Does it strike you as unusual that the water is described as 'simple'? Is it really the water that is simple?

[c] What Caribbean historical experience do stanzas 6, 7, and 8 try to suggest? Who is the poet pretending to be in these stanzas?

[d] Look at the beginning of stanzas 1, 4 and 9. How do you describe the stylistic feature you see? What function does it serve in stanza 9?

[e] Who is the poet pretending to be from stanza 10 to the end of the poem?

[f] Are all the stanzas in the poem of equal length? Which is different? Why? What is the effect of the line 'I watched him pause'? What does the poet suggest Columbus was feeling?

[g] What does 'splashing silence' bring to your imagination? What does the *sound* of the words of the last three lines suggest to you?

[h] Why, would you say, are the sentences and words broken up as they are? Do you think the lines could have been set down in a different way? Try setting out some of the lines in a different way and see whether a different arrangement gives the same rhythm and feeling.

THESE GOLDEN MOMENTS (p 6)

[a] Written poetry as a form of art grew out of the art of song when bards sang to entertain audiences. What songs are meant in this extract? In what way are they related to 'golden moments'? What makes them golden? What is 'the gold that flows'?

[b] What has caused the singing in this case? Why, do you judge, is sanity connected with the singing?

[c] Are the images of these lines concrete or abstract, strong or weak? Give your reasons for your judgment or reaction.

Narrative Poems

Narrative poems tell stories. And although it is true that story is only one of the elements that help to give the total experience of a poem, it is useful to concentrate initially on the story element in the poems in this section. It is worth examining how each writer organises his story—the extent to which our grasp of the action depends upon the introduction of dramatic scenes, speech, and the descriptions of people, places or objects. Such an examination leads into and helps us to answer the more basic question as to why the poet chooses to tell a particular story; what interests, in addition to or apart from 'telling a good story', the poem serves; and what feelings it arouses in us.

Almost thirty years separate Cruickshank's *Hard Luck* and McNeill's *The True Gage*. This group of poems, therefore, allows us to observe certain broad patterns in the development of West Indian poetry. The middle class trivia of Una Marson (with nothing to say, and hardly a story to tell) are succeeded by the controlled and seemingly impersonal expression of strong feeling in the gripping stories of Morris and McNeill. Alma Norman's *Revolt of Chief Tacky* belongs to two new developments in West Indian poetry: the attempt to make West Indian history something to be proud of; and the deliberate beginning of a literature in the islands written specifically for children. The West Indian poet's confidence about his West Indian-ness, his sense of freedom now from the nationalist impulse to "West-Indianise" his material in obvious ways, is illustrated by the poems of Morris and McNeill, as well as in the refusal of Derek Walcott to exploit or stress the exotic possibilities of his folk-lore material in *Le Loupgarou*.

HENRY'S AMBITION (*p* 8)

[*a*] What was Henry's ambition? Did it surprise you to discover this? What evidence is there that the author wants to surprise the reader?

[*b*] In normal prose the second sentence of this poem would be patterned like this: 'You would think he was ambitious to be a sailor man.' Does this mean that in writing verse you must change the normal pattern of sentences?

[c] Compare the line endings in this poem with those in *Road-Mending*. Do you think poems without rhyme are less enjoyable than poems with rhyme?

[d] What is your attitude to Henry? What do you think is the author's attitude to him? Point to parts and features of the poem to explain your answer.

HARD LUCK (*p* 9)

[a] Give the lawyer's argument in your own words. What is your attitude to people who speak in the way the lawyer does? Do you think that this is the author's attitude to such people too? Support your opinion with evidence from the poem.

[b] *Hard Luck* and *Henry's Ambition* tell stories. Which one tells its story more quickly? Is the author of *Hard Luck* interested in more than just telling a story? Why does such a large part of the poem deal with the lawyer's antics? Why is the poem called *Hard Luck*?

[c] What do you enjoy most in this poem—the story, the rhyme, or the mood? Make some comments on one or more of those three.

REVOLT OF CHIEF TACKY (*p* 12)

[a] What did Tacky do? Did he succeed in his aim? If not, why not?

[b] Why are the lines at the end of each stanza put into brackets? In reading the poem, what ought to be done with the lines in brackets? Can anything else be done with this poem besides reading it aloud?

[c] Look again at the lines in brackets. How does each relate to the line that precedes it? Is there any exception to the pattern? What is the effect of this exception?

[d] Is this a poem that celebrates or a poem that mourns? What or who is being celebrated or mourned?

THE POND (*p* 13)

[a] What did the old people say of the pond?

[b] 'Drawn so hard by prohibitions.' What does this mean? Have you ever been drawn by prohibitions? Give an instance or two.

[c] How did the boy get to the pond?

[d] Why was the pond dark and mysterious when he got there?

[*e*] Again we have a strange ending to what appears to be a simple story-poem. Which of these, if any, is the poet telling us in this poem?
  (i) imagined fears disappear when faced;
  (ii) old people frighten children with stories to keep them from danger;
  (iii) the source of all evil is in ourselves.
Explain why you chose (i), (ii), or (iii), or why you chose neither.

[*f*] When you read this poem aloud (as you should do all poems over and over) what makes it sound like ordinary conversational speech? What makes it sound different from ordinary conversational speech?

[*g*] What phrases of the poem do you find most interesting? Give your reasons in each case.

THE VISIT (*p* 14)

[*a*] Since a horse must leave hoofprints, in line 25 'hoofprints' is being used to mean something else, to make a comparison. What could the comparison be?

[*b*] If 'hoofprints' is used to mean something else, the following words are also being used metaphorically—'town' (line 6); 'dung' (line 9); 'worms' (line 15); 'great birds' (line 18); 'echoes' (line 24). What could be meant in each case?

[*c*] Considering the use of the word 'indifferent' (line 25) in what sense or senses was the 'town' dead? In what way was the stranger a stranger?

[*d*] The stranger 'raised no echoes', the town was 'dead' and 'great birds' glided in. What do these phrases point to with regard to:
  (i) who or what the stranger was;
  (ii) who or what the great birds were?

[*e*] Considering the music made by the bird, the keskidee, and that the whole poem seems to be a metaphor or comparison, who or what could the keskidee represent? Who notices the keskidee? Why?

[*f*] What tone of voice do you hear with these words: 'formal' (line 11); 'patience' (line 13); 'jaws' (line 19)? What do you receive from them of the poet's attitude and meaning?

[*g*] Explore the associations that go with each of these and consider their place in the poem: lianas, brambles, ticking clock, stable.

[*h*] Ernest Hemingway's story, *A Clean Well-Lighted Place*, has a prostitute as its central character. Does this have anything to do with the poem, do you think, or did the poet happen to use the phrase because he liked it?

THE CASTLE (*p* 15)

[a] Who (or what, perhaps) is 'that king who terrifies us all'?

[b] Why are his courtiers and his court described as 'yellow'? What is the colour 'yellow' being used to represent in this poem?

[c] The knight is described at first as 'the bold knight' then 'this honourable knight' then 'the giddy knight' and finally just 'the knight'. What does each phrase in turn suggest about the author's attitude to the knight, and in what way do you think the progression from 'the bold knight' to 'the knight' is significant?

[d] What possible connection can you find between the death of the knight and the inscription on the wall: 'Living is fearing'?

[e] In what sort of story do we usually get words like 'castle', 'courtiers', 'court', 'knight', 'flag' and 'moat'?

[f] With what kind of story do we associate the rhythm and rhyme of this poem?

[g] What would you say *The Castle* is really about?

LE LOUPGAROU (*p* 16)

[a] Is this another story-poem? How much of it tells a story?

[b] What is the story of Le Brun? What bargains do you imagine he had made?

[c] What does the phrase 'slowly shutting jalousies' suggest to you about what is going on behind the jalousies?

[d] To whom does the poet refer as 'Christian witches'? Why? What does the phrase tell you about his attitude to them?

[e] Is this poem as easy to read as *Henry's Ambition* or *Hard Luck*? Would you say that such difficulties as there may be lie mainly in the vocabulary, the kinds of sentence the poet uses, the rhythm, or the ideas? Are difficult poems less enjoyable than easy ones such as *Henry's Ambition*?

[f] Study the rhyme scheme and the division of the poem into sections which it suggests. Have you come across this kind of patterning before, or elsewhere in this book? Is there any connection between the arrangement into sections and the arrangement of the ideas in the poem?

THE TRUE GAGE (*p* 17)

[a] What do you imagine when you read that the room 'proceeded to grow around him'? What experience is the poet trying to suggest? Does what you imagine when you read 'hearing the walls like temples around his ears' support your view?

[b] What do you think the 'he' of the poem does in the final stanza?
Does the line about taking 'a gun or a ruler' make sense to you?
How does it tie in with different associations of the word 'gage'?

[c] What do you think is the poet's attitude to the man's action?
What emotions does the story arouse in you?

TO A CRIPPLED SCHOOLMASTER (p 18)

[a] Who are the 'we' referred to by the poet?

[b] What do these phrases suggest to you about the schoolmaster, and
about the feeling of the group towards him: 'Drag slower and
slower'; 'When body couldn't serve your eager will'; and
'A special house to cage you in'?

[c] At what point in the poem does the poet begin to concentrate on
'I' rather than 'we'? About how old do you imagine the separated
'I' to be?

[d] What is the predominant mood of the 'I' in stanzas 5, 6, and 7?
What changes have come over him, and what does 'Time has
stolen' suggest about his attitude to these changes?

[e] 'But the fear of facing death'. Whose fear? The death of whom
or what?

[f] Is this a poem about the schoolmaster's decay, or changes that have
taken place in the 'I', or both? Give reasons for your conclusion.

[g] Nearly all the stanzas in this poem consist of a single sentence.
Find the one exception. Can you think of reasons why the poet
does this?

JAFFO THE CALYPSONIAN (p 19)

[a] Enumerate all the 'facts' of Jaffo's life given in the poem. What
force do these 'facts' have on you?

[b] Do you think the poet was more interested in awakening your
sympathy for Jaffo or in giving you a realisation of the strength of
Jaffo's obsession? Argue the matter with quotations from the poem.

[c] What kind of image and feeling do you get from each of these?
    (i) ragged still-eyed men;
    (ii) the look of unsung calypsoes stared in his eyes;
    (iii) rat-trap rum shops;
    (iv) respectable eyes.

[*d*] The poet puts certain phrases together for the kind of sounds the words have, as well as for other reasons. What effects or suggestions do you hear from the sounds in these phrases?

  (i) clogged throat;

  (ii) sang and sang with staccato shout;

  (iii) thickened to a hard final silence;

  (iv) grated in brassy fear.

[*e*] Can you detect the beat and rhythm of the poet's language in this poem? Does it have any resemblance or relation to the subject matter of the poem? If so, explain the relationship. Does it fit or contrast with Jaffo's fate? What reason could the poet have had for using it?

Dialect into Poetry

The tendency to associate dialect with 'comic', 'simple', 'pathetic' or 'vulgar' is, or used to be, very strong in the West Indies. When West Indian writers began to use dialect in their works, the educated middle-class resistance to it usually took the form that it was 'bad' English and not suitable for books. Everybody knew, but nobody liked to say, that behind the shame of 'bad' English was the embarrassment caused by the stereotypes of the Black Man and the peasant which dialect seemed to call up.

In the last twenty years, the West Indian novelist has gone ahead and used dialect to express such complex emotions in such tangled human situations that the peasant language is being increasingly recognised as a major stylistic resource. Although West Indian poets have only just begun to follow the novelists in exploiting the concrete, vivid, rhythmic effects latent in dialect, there have been dialect poems since the early years of the century. Nearly all the poems in Claude McKay's *Constab Ballads* (1912) are in dialect (McKay used to be called 'the Bobby Burns of Jamaica'), and Tom Redcam, whose *A Market Basket in the Car* appears here, wrote a number of serious dialect poems too. But both McKay and Redcam confine themselves to using dialect for a social realism, that is, to give a picture of people and situations just as they appear in everyday life. Louise Bennett advances beyond this simple use of dialect, and makes great use of its incisiveness and wit in her comments on the Jamaican scene. But enjoyable as she is in performance, Louise Bennett's range is often restricted to topicality and journalism; it is only with the emergence of Edward Brathwaite that what is nowadays being called 'the folk speech' comes into its own as a literary medium to be stretched and coiled and tuned in West Indian poetry without any need being felt simply to reproduce dialect as it is spoken. Brathwaite and Scott use dialect to express sombre themes in the poems included here, and Hendriks deflates the language and attitudes of his old woman by the skilful introduction of dialect rhythms at the end of his poem.

In many of the poems in this collection, especially the later ones, it is necessary to hear the author's voice as a West Indian voice. If this is done it may be possible to begin to understand how dialect rhythms and intonations belong to West Indian poems even when the poem does not seem to the eye to be related to dialect at all.

Hendriks' poem, in which the old woman's pretentiousness is done in British English, her everyday self in Jamaican Standard English, and her annoyed self in a form of dialect, is a good example of the linguistic possibilities open to the West Indian poet.

A MARKET BASKET IN THE CAR (p 22)

[a] The car mentioned here is a tram-car which you may have seen only pictures of. What is the mood of the speaker? What caused him/her to get into this mood? What social class do you imagine the speaker to come from?

[b] What common beliefs and attitudes come out in the second stanza? What present-day ideas are being used to get rid of them?

[c] What amuses you in the poem? Why does it amuse?

[d] What comment can you make on the literary value of the line: 'While I drop you out a me eye?'

[e] 'The poem is in a dialect or patois language and therefore is not to be taken seriously'. Do you agree with this statement? Give your reasons for agreeing or disagreeing.

COLONISATION IN REVERSE (p 23)

[a] Colonisation may be described as the invasion of a people's land by another people and the taking of its riches. What actual movement of people is the poet writing about?

[b] Explain 'An tun history upside dung'. In what ways, if any, does the title fit the poem?

[c] Do you think the writer approves of the emigration described in the poem? How do you know?

[d] 'But fe show dem loyalty'. Does the poet really mean this? In what way do you take the phrase?

[e] What problem does the poet pose in the final stanza? How apt is the reference to war?

[f] After reading the poem aloud, turn back to *Revolt of Chief Tacky* and read that out. What differences or similarities do you notice in the rhythm? Which poem do you prefer from this point of view and why?

[g] Discuss any evidence of irony which you find in the poem.

from THE DUST (*p* 25)

[*a*] This too is a poem in dialect. Does the tone of voice of the poet suggest (i) laughter and amusement (ii) sneering and jeering or (iii) sadness and regret? When you have decided, tell what it is, as expressed in the poem, that makes him feel that way.

[*b*] What signs of youth and strength are given in the poem? What signs of age and infirmity? Why, in each case?

[*c*] Compare this poem with *To a Crippled Schoolmaster* in theme, mood and treatment.

[*d*] What organises the language of the poem, apart from rhyme, to make it different from loose everyday talk?

[*e*] Does the fact that the poem is written in dialect help or hinder you in getting the feeling of what the poem means?

[*f*] What effect does the last line of the poem have on you?

UNCLE TIME (*p* 27)

[*a*] Read the poem several times to familiarise yourself with its dialect rhythm.

[*b*] Who is Uncle Time? What is the poem about? Is it a serious or a frivolous theme?

[*c*] What different characteristic of Uncle Time is predominant in each stanza? How do the following phrases help to impress these characteristics upon the reader: 'scraping away de lan' (stanza 1); 'is a spider-man' (stanza 2); and 'smile black as sorrow' (stanza 3)?

[*d*] Pick out some of the images that convey strong sense impressions and discuss whether or how much these contribute to the meaning of the poem.

[*e*] Does the poem derive strength or weakness from the use of familiar local objects, e.g. wet sand, mongoose, bamboo leaf, cane-fire, cassava? Does the use of dialect reduce or increase the seriousness or frivolousness of the poem?

[*f*] What is the dominant mood of the poem? Apart from the sense, what feature of the poem conveys this mood to you?

AN OLD JAMAICAN WOMAN THINKS ABOUT THE HEREAFTER (p 28)

[a] What big place is referred to in the first line?

[b] What feelings or ideas do you associate with the things the old woman wants?

[c] What picture does the poem make you imagine or remember? What feelings, if any, do you associate with such pictures?

[d] What impressions do you get of the old Jamaican woman in the first 21 lines of the poem? What impression of her do you get in the last three lines? How do the last three lines differ in tone when you read the poem aloud?

[e] What is the effect of having so many monosyllables in the last three lines? In what way is this device appropriate, especially when compared with the earlier part of the poem?

[f] Is this poem a dialect poem in the way the three preceding poems are? What do the four poems in this section suggest to you about the use of dialect in poetry? Consider this question under the following headings: subject matter; range of emotions and degree of seriousness/comicality.

Nature and Landscape: Trees

In his introduction to *Themes of Song: An Anthology of Guianese Poetry* (1961), A. J. Seymour speaks of 'many poems depicting the beauty of Nature around us', and praises poets because they 'make us see that around us there are many sights and sounds of beauty, if we would only stop, and stand, and look, and listen.' A great deal of early West Indian poetry was too simply concerned with observing Beauty and contemplating Nature. Instead of involving us in their response to the world around them, the poets sought to tell us about what they saw by using what they regarded as 'poetic' words, adding an elevated 'poetic' thought for us to take away. The poets very often saw it as part of the game not only to use 'poetic' words and 'elevated' thoughts but also to cast their poems in highly regular metrical patterns and stanza forms. Tom Redcam's *Now the Lignum Vitae Blows* is included here to illustrate this and to help us mark what West Indian poetry developed away from. Redcam's poem gives the impression of a mechanical imitation of models only half understood. McKay's *Castaways*, which follows, has an obvious foot in this school, but McKay manages to use the sonnet form to swing the poem away from the empty contemplation of landscape towards an awareness of the destitution of the people in that landscape.

Nature continues to be a dominant strain in West Indian poetry. Nature in modern West Indian poetry, however, makes itself felt as a landscape whose features symbolise the problems and possibilities of life in these islands; and instead of general reflections we find expressed a sensuous response to this landscape. Derek Walcott, for instance, the outstanding example of this tradition, evokes his landscape with vividness and precision. This quality of evocation, and the accompanying sense of a mind seeking to find meanings in life, mark the emergence of West Indian poetry from Nature poems like Redcam's. Walcott's *In a Green Night* makes us see an orange tree more vividly than ever, but it can hardly be described as a poem about an orange tree.

NOW THE LIGNUM VITAE BLOWS (*p* 30)

[*a*] Which of these gives a concrete particular picture and which a general one:
  (i) 'Fair-browed April enters here'
  (ii) 'the Brown Bee comes and goes'.
Which do you think is more effective and why? What other examples can you find of (i) and (ii) in the poem?

[*b*] What does the sound of the first four lines in the second stanza suggest to you? What gives the lines that suggestive sound?

[*c*] How does this poem attempt to capture the essence of the season of year it describes? Does it succeed?

[*d*] Does 'mystic loom' suggest anything specific to you? Why does the poet repeat the line in which this phrase occurs?

[*e*] How regular is the versification in this poem? What is the effect of this regularity upon you?

THE CASTAWAYS (*p* 31)

[*a*] What kind of scene does the poet evoke in the first seven lines? What does this lead you to expect the poem to be about? At what point do you realise that your expectations will not be met?

[*b*] Who are the Castaways referred to? How does the poet feel about them? What, do you imagine, is meant by 'life's shadows dark and deep'?

[*c*] If the poet's concern is for the 'castaways', are the first seven lines irrelevant? How do they contribute to the poet's effectiveness in drawing attention to the sufferers in the poem?

[*d*] What is the basic contrast being used by the poet, and why does he use it?

[*e*] Are 'vivid grass', 'butterflies', 'sparrows', 'dandelions', 'rare daffodils', and 'thrushes' subjects or objects of the verb 'behold'? Is this what one would have expected on reading the first seven lines? What purpose does the poet's inversion of normal sentence structure serve? Do you think that poets should invert normal sentence structures as a general rule? Does this automatically make lines poetic?

[*f*] Into how many units does the poem divide according to punctuation? See if each section is concerned with something particular to itself. How do the sections relate to each other?

[*g*] Compare McKay's arrangement of the sonnet form with Walcott's in *Le Loupgarou*.

[*a*] What picture does the first stanza evoke for you? What does the poet refer to as 'perfected fables' and why?

[*b*] Does the phrase 'Last season's summer height' mean any of these:
  (i) last season's sun
  (ii) the height of the tree during the summer of her last year of fruit-bearing life
  (iii) that the previous season was summer and the tree stood at its highest then?

[*c*] Make a mental picture of what is exposed when all the leaves fall from a tree. Does this suggest to you any ways in which a tree is like other living things, including people? With your answers to these questions in mind put in your own words the statement that the poet is making about appearance and reality in stanza two.

[*d*] What do you think are the splendours referred to in line 12? What feeds these splendours? What quails them?

[*e*] What does the poet tell us about the different effects of dew and dust on the appearance of the orange:
  (i) at an early stage, and
  (ii) at a later stage in its development?

[*f*] What do you imagine as happening when you are told that the tree sought to surpass the mottling of the rust all summer?

[*g*] What do you understand by 'cyclic chemistry that dooms and glories her at once'?

[*h*] Do stanzas 5, 6 and 7 deal with the orange tree in the same way that the earlier stanzas do? What does the poet compare with the orange tree in stanza 5? What is the basis of this comparison?

[*i*] What impression do the phrases 'loud with citron leaves' and 'crystal falls to heal' suggest to you about the place called Florida in the poem? Citron is the bitter rind of a variety of grapefruit artificially sweetened and used as a confectionery. Does this information alter in any way your impression of Florida? In connection with this, pay attention to the sound of the word 'falls' and the associations which go with 'crystal'.

[*j*] What does 'loss of visionary rage' mean? What kind of person would you say suffers such a loss? Does the poet think that it is possible to fool ourselves about this kind of loss? If the answer is no, what would you say the poem offers as an alternative? What do you understand by the phrase 'the comprehending heart'?

[*k*] What causes the blight in line 25? Is it a physical blight or a blight on the spirit? What then would you say 'Time's fires' means? Is the poet referring to his own art in line 26? If so, what is he saying about it?

[*l*] What is the relationship, if any, between 'comfortable creed' of line 10 and 'lampless night' of line 27?

[*m*] What is the difference between stanza 1 and stanza 8? Why do you think the poet introduces this difference? What is 'that fable' of this final stanza?

TELL ME TREES: WHAT ARE YOU WHISPERING? (*p* 33)

[*a*] The speaker of this poems seems to be in love with trees. Why? Have you ever had a feeling resembling this wish to be part of the vegetation or buildings around you?

[*b*] 'I and the leaves shall always lie together'. When does the poet say this will happen? What does this indicate about his attitude to death? Does the use of the words 'green', 'fresh', and 'sweet' further your understanding of the poet's attitude to death?

[*c*] What effect does the repetition of lines containing 'leaves' have on you? What sort of occasion do you associate with such repetition? How does the word 'robe' connect with all this?

[*d*] Are the trees in this poem used in the same way and for the same purpose as the orange trees in *In a Green Night*?

The Line of Literary Resistance

In the Preface to Martin Carter's *Poems of Resistance* (University of Guyana, 1964), Neville Dawes describes Carter's poems as being 'in a line of literary resistance which may be said to begin with Claude McKay of Jamaica'. The 'line of literary resistance' is the second major phase of West Indian poetry (of which *Road-mending* has already been described as part). This phase includes poems of protest and defiance about the condition of the Negro, such as Carter's *I come from the Nigger Yard* which opens:

I come from the nigger yard of yesterday
leaping from the oppressor's hate
and the scorn of myself;
from the agony of the dark hut in the shadow
and the hurt of things;
from the long days of cruelty and the long nights of pain
down to the wide streets of tomorrow, of the next day
leaping I come, who cannot see will hear.

The phase also includes poems like *Carnival Rhapsody* in which the much less accomplished Knolly S. LaFortune anticipates Edward Brathwaite in seeking to unite dialect and rhythmic drums as part of a creative groping out of suffering and self-contempt:

Beat dem drums
Boys beat dem drums
Fast and loud and sweet
Dey go ge we consolation,
Dey go ease we sufferation,
Down Frederick Street,
Down Frederick Street.

And in *Ancestor on the Auction Block*, Africa and the slave past are even more directly invoked: Vera Bell sees the West Indian's need to come to terms with the slave past as the prerequisite for the birth of a new society in the islands. The legacy of shame must be accepted and translated, however painful the first bold embrace:

Ancestor on the auction block
Across the years your eyes seek mine
Compelling me to look.

I see your shackled feet
Your primitive black face
I see your humiliation
And turn away
Ashamed.

A less obvious aspect of this phase in West Indian poetry may be illustrated by A. M. Clarke's *The Rice Planters*:

The Mermaids rose from out the water into the glare
Shaking their hair
From drops of brown muddy water,

and P.M. Sherlock's only too well-known *Jamaican Fisherman*, in both of which the poets look at the despised peasant type with idealising intent.

Not many of the poems belonging to 'the line of literary resistance' strike us today as of much interest on the stylistic or imaginative levels. But the issues raised in them have come up again in the late 1960s, especially in the accomplished work of the Barbadian, Edward Brathwaite; and at least one important voice was turning radicalism into poetry in the earlier period: the Guyanese, Martin Carter, is recognised in this anthology by the inclusion of five of his poems written before he became a successful politician.

It would be misleading, however, to leave the impression that only protest poetry was being written by West Indians in the 1930s and 1940s. The poet's imagination travels beyond what is socially realistic in some of Carter's finer poems; and in A. J. Seymour's *There Runs a Dream* (which is included here), a meditation on the Guyanese rivers and jungles opens up into a reflection on people, place and history in Guyana, deepening in the second stanza into an intimation of what Time does to human effort. A more obviously metaphysical strain appears in the poetry of Wilson Harris (Guyana), and in that of the Jamaicans, Roger Mais, George Campbell and M. G. Smith. Smith's poem about the painfulness of imaginative creativity, *These Golden Moments* (included in the opening section of this anthology), and his poem called *The Land* are both grounded upon the writer's social and cultural awareness, but can hardly be called socially realistic. It is only when we take account of this relatively neglected metaphysical aspect of early West Indian poetry that we can fully appreciate what lies behind *The Falls*, one of the finest poems in Derek Walcott's *The Gulf* (1970), where it appears in the 'Guyana' sequence:

Their barrelling roar would open like a white oven
for him,
who was a spirit now, who could not burn or drown.

Surely in that 'smoke that thundered' there was a door—
but the noise boiled to the traffic of a white town
of bicycles, pigeons, bells, smoke, trains at the rush hour

revolving to this roar.
He was a flower,
weightless. He would float down.

from DEATH OF A SLAVE (*p* 36)

[*a*] What experiences of a slave does the poet make you feel or
imagine? Select lines or phrases which help this, and say how they
help.

[*b*] Have you ever seen the white birds that follow the beasts of the
field? What do the white birds of stanza 3 signify? Why are they
like dreams?

[*c*] Why is night 'like a thief'? (line 15)

[*d*] What does the silence of the slave's drum seem to symbolise, if
anything?

[*e*] What do you understand by the seeds of anger planted in the
earth? Into what do you think they will grow?

[*f*] Does this obsession with slavery seem healthy and genuine to you
or does it suggest the false refuge of a mind insensitive to present
experience? Argue the matter.

THIS IS THE DARK TIME, MY LOVE (*p* 37)

[*a*] This poem was written when the freedom of British Guiana was
'suspended' in 1953 and British soldiers policed the country.
What phrase in the second stanza tells why it is 'the dark time'?
What events, according to the poem, are taking place in 'the dark
time'?

[*b*] What do you think the poet means by 'brown beetles' (line 2):
'red flowers' (line 4): 'the stranger invader' (line 11): and 'your
dream' (line 12)?

[*c*] What effect or force do these phrases have for you?
(i) festival of guns (line 7);
(ii) carnival of misery (line 7);
(iii) aiming at your dream (line 12).

TILL I COLLECT (p 38)

[a] In terms of visual imagery what scene is painted for you and what feelings come over your spirit from the scene? What specially helps to convey those feelings?

[b] What significance do these words seem to have in the poem: 'blood' (line 1); 'anguish' (line 5); 'bones' (line 12); 'resurrect' (line 12); 'scattered skeleton' (line 17)?

[c] In what sense is the poet looking back? What is he looking back to?

[d] Do any of these comparisons bring pleasure to you? If so, try to say what you enjoy from them:
  (i) the moon is blood;
  (ii) the fence of lights;
  (iii) my rudder tempered out of anguish;
  (iv) strain the liquid billow;
  (v) the islands of the stars.

THERE RUNS A DREAM (p 39)

[a] What dream do the rivers contain in stanza one? How do 'lost stellings', 'trim dwellings', and 'fields of indigo' contribute to our picture of what that dream was?

[b] What is the river's knowledge? Do the phrase 'Strong and quiet men' and the rest of stanza two alter your view of the men you imagine in stanza one? In what ways? How does stanza two 'interpret' the more historical stanza one?

[c] Explain or comment on the phrase 'history moved down river'.

THIS LAND (p 40)

[a] What interpretation do you put upon 'the voice' (line 2) and 'the flame' (line 5)? What guides you in your interpretation?

[b] What do you infer that the island is waiting for (lines 22 to 27)? What makes you think so?

[c] Who do you think is doing the weeping and the bleating? Why?

[d] How has repetition helped this poem to achieve its effect? What general effect does the poem have on your imagination?

[e] What comment, if any, would you make on the level of the comparisons employed in the poem—are they striking, familiar but interesting, stale, original, weak, simple, complex, or what? Explain the reason for your personal reaction.

SHEEP (p 41)

[a] Which set of lines present to your imagination the more vivid image—lines 2 to 6 or lines 7 to 10?

[b] What, do you suppose, made the poet write this poem?

[c] In what parts of the poem does the poet use the sounds of words to get an effect? Does this help the feeling in the poem or not?

[d] In what way does the last line give a new depth to the poem?

Voices

There was almost as much bad poetry arising from the West Indian poets' concentration on socio-economic themes as from the earlier writers' idyllic contemplation of Nature. The great shift in the subject matter of West Indian poetry was accompanied by changed attitudes to language and style: the regular patterns and rigid stanza forms gave way to freer rhythms closer to the speaking voice; the stilted poetic words of the early poems began to be replaced by a more wide-ranging vocabulary that could include the simple, the harsh or the vulgar as the particular poem demanded; and instead of offering pompous generalisations about Life or Death or Beauty the poet began to explore and express his own experiences, his own way of seeing and feeling.

There are signs of all this in the second phase of West Indian poetry, but the successes seem to come in single poems from authors whose names we seldom remember. One hardly gets the impression of a poet with a vision of his own that is being explored and followed from one moment of experience to another; or of an artist to whom language presented itself as a dynamic medium to work in, work with or work upon. There were poets with grouses, and perhaps poets like M. G. Smith with dreams and visions, but there was as yet, with the possible exception of Martin Carter, no poet with the imagination and the intimacy with language that are prerequisites for possessing a voice.

This part of the anthology is dominated by poems by Derek Walcott and Edward Brathwaite, the two West Indian poets with established reputations; and poems by a number of new writers whose work has yet to appear in their own collections: Mervyn Morris, Wayne Brown, Anthony McNeill and Dennis Scott. The emergence of these new writers, conscious of one another and of their predecessors and older contemporaries, and writing in a variety of styles about a wide range of experience, more than confirms that West Indian poetry has reached a critical point in its development. There will always be the impressive single poem produced in an inspired spell by an amateur, but the age of the dedicated practitioner, ruled by his imagination or vision, and conscious of craft, has arrived. It is hoped that the poems here will reveal both the differences and the continuities within the period from Walcott to Brathwaite, and will indicate the new directions in which they may lead.

108

The poems in this section also illustrate the most persistent element in West Indian poetry—the tradition of looking at the landscape. The arrangement in clusters helps to reveal this continuity, marking broad developments in West Indian poetry, and suggesting differences between individual poets. The group called 'Trees' has already been used to suggest a wide range of attitudes and styles and major changes in West Indian poetry. 'Cats' offers contrasts in style (metre, rhythm, symbolism etc.), and helps us to understand the relationship between style and attitude. *The Cat* is a charming exercise in observation and unobtrusive technical control. Brathwaite's *Leopard*, pacing the island-rocks and unable to pounce, is a charged symbol of West Indian frustration and stifled energy. In 'Birds' and 'Fish', recent poems by Scott and Brown offer illuminating comparison with older works by Lucie-Smith and Seymour. (These examples are intended to recommend to student and teacher a way of using the dates provided in conjunction with the poems themselves. As the reader moves through the collection, it should be possible for him to understand and analyse developments in West Indian poetry without taking the Editors' suggestions as authority.)

The poems have also been arranged to suggest a physical environment, the elements at work upon it, and an impression of a living people. The group 'Learning' suggests the process of growing up—from childhood, through death and loss, to reflections on innocence and experience. In addition to the primary emphasis on the disconcerting experience of figures finding themselves suddenly exposed, there is in the group 'Lost Leaders' an implicit comment on political leadership in the West Indies. The two departure poems, *New World A-Comin'* and *Pages from a Journal, 1834*, are not specifically about the emigration of West Indians to England and America in this century (the former deals with the slave voyage, the latter with the white West Indian's withdrawal at the time of Emancipation); but they are expressions of a similar sense of unwilling removal. The exile poems are expressive of malaise (*The Harlem Dancer*), alienation (*The Room*) and the nostalgia (*Kite-Flying* and *I shall Return*) that are part of the modern West Indian experience of emigration.

'The Return' begins with *South* which comes from Brathwaite's *Rights of Passage*. *South* exults in a return to the islands at last after years of painful wandering in alien climes and after a self-discovering pilgrimage to West Africa. The poem implies that after his experiences abroad, the West Indian must return to see his island, its people and its possibilities from a new perspective. *Squatter's Rites*, *Ancestors* and *Who's Sammy?* are examples of writing from such a new perspective. Only one of the three poets has made the physical and imaginative journey to West Africa, but all three poems deal with traditionally despised elements in West Indian society. In *Ogun* the reader is invited to look with imaginative eyes sharpened by a sense of history, in order to recognise in the village carpenter an African craftsman. But *Ogun* is much more satisfying as a myth of creation (a celebration of creative possibilities in these islands). Its triumphant mood complements the resolution of *The Knife of Dawn* and the hesitant closure of *Allegre*, a poem about the birth and creation of a nation and of a self, too.

THE CAT (*p* 44)

[a] How representative of a cat's actions is this description? What words and phrases indicate to you that the writer has observed the cat very closely?

[b] What is the poet's attitude to the cat? What words and phrases help to indicate this attitude most clearly?

[c] Does a cat smile? What made the poet imagine a 'voluptuous slow smile'?

[d] Does the writer mean this particular cat was once worshipped near the Nile? If not what do you think he might be saying?

[e] Putting aside, as far as you can, the actual meanings of the words, how does the shape of the sentence 'Pleasures . . . tail' help you to experience the feeling it expresses?

[f] Why, do you suppose, the poem is divided into two groups of eight and six lines respectively? How do the two groups differ?

from LEOPARD (*p* 45)

[a] How does the description of the leopard of this poem compare with that of the cat in the previous poem?

[b] Pick out some of the words and phrases that seem to you to suggest most effectively the condition of the leopard. How does the positioning of these words and phrases affect their impact? What other devices does the poet use to impress the condition of the leopard upon us?

[c] Where is the leopard? Why is he suffering?

[d] How does the phrase 'water ringing in the islands' doubt' affect your understanding of the phrase 'cage of glint, rock'? What then is this leopard caught in?

[e] How do you interpret the phrase 'islands' doubt'? What does 'doubt' suggest about the state of the islands or islanders? What could the uncertainty be about? How does it connect with 'cage' and 'strike no glory'?

[f] Is the poet interested in the leopard merely as leopard or as a symbol? Try to answer an imaginary questioner who wants to know what the poem is really about.

[g] Write out the substance of the poem in a few sentences of your own and then compare your prose version with the poem. Which has the greater appeal? Why?

A COMFORT OF CROWS (p 46)

[a] What kind of place is meant by 'here' in the poem?

[b] The phrase 'even here' is used twice in the poem. What is the poet implying when he uses 'even'?

[c] What offers solace and comfort? In what way?

[d] What does 'ceremonies' refer to? How appropriate is the word? Is there any similarity between the way 'ceremonies' is used and the way 'highways' and 'kindness' are?

[e] Explain briefly in your own words what the poet is asking us to mark or notice.

[f] Looking at subject matter, imagery and mood, what similarities and differences can you find between this poem and *Carrion Crows*?

CARRION CROWS (p 47)

[a] What is carrion? What ideas are usually associated with carrion crows? Are any of these used in the poem?

[b] What impression of the crows do the following phrases help to convey: 'brooding with evil eyes'; 'feast on swollen carrion'; and 'pestered by flies'?

[c] What seems to be the poet's attitude to the crows in the first six lines?

[d] The ninth line begins with 'But'. What does this lead you to expect? What impression of the crows does the poet convey in the last six lines? What words and phrases help to give this impression? Is the poet's attitude to the crows a different one now? In what sense, if at all, are the two attitudes consistent with each other?

[e] Read the last six lines again. Suppose that instead of these lines the writer had said: 'But I have also seen them flying around and their shadows passing over the fields.' Would that have been as vivid to you? Give your reasons.

PELICANS (p 48)

[a] St Simeon Stylites sat on a high pillar fasting for thirty years. Why are the pelicans called stylite pelicans?

[b] In what respects does the poet show the pelican as resembling a saint?

[c] What changes its apparent saintliness?

[d] What does the pelican then reveal of himself?

[e] Does this use of contrast make the poem better for you, or does it tend to spoil the picture? In what way?

[f] Is the use of contrast in this poem more striking or less so than in *The Castaways*?

[g] What is unusual in the image 'deserts of the bay'? Is it an effective image? Why?

[h] Comment on the use of the words 'glitters' and 'rewarded' so close to each other. How does this affect the way you visualise the shoal of fish?

BIRD (p 49)

[a] What do you imagine from line 2? How does the repetition of the word 'and' help to convey the impression?

[b] What literary device is used in line 5? Do you think it serves any useful purpose in this part of the poem?

[c] Why do you think the poet has described the bird at such length?

[d] Why did the boy's throat grow tight with warning?

[e] What strikes you about lines 13 and 14? Why are they put before 'Yes, there'?

[f] Look at these phrases: 'slow day'; 'steep sky'; and 'feathered morning'. What strikes you about these combinations of words? Find other instances of unusual combinations in the poem.

[g] Was it the sun that made the boy's eyes run? What difference is there between the two boys?

[h] In what ways do the first ten lines differ from the rest of the poem? The use of the word 'Oh' is one of the clues to a quality you may not have thought about.

[i] What change is there in the manner of presentation after line 10? How would you describe the latter section? How appropriate and effective do you think it is?

MACKEREL (*p* 50)

[*a*] What forms the action in Part 1 of the poem? What did the mackerel do? Pick out phrases in each of the four stanzas which help you to point to the poet's interpretation of the action. (As a start you may consider 'on a casual quest, forgetting time'.) If someone did a painting to illustrate this part of the poem what would you expect to see in it?

[*b*] What action is there in Part 2 of the poem? If there is no action in the sense that there is action in Part 1, how would you describe what is given in the second part of the poem?

[*c*] What makes the poet imagine a final fate for the mackerel? What is his attitude to people who do this (including himself)? Explain what in lines 30–33 helps you to understand his attitude.

[*d*] 'The curiosity of a child and a child's horror'. What, do you think, causes the 'horror' and why is it described as 'a child's horror'? Discuss whether the phrase successfully conveys the poet's feelings at this stage about what he has seen.

[*e*] Attempt a paraphrase of the last 8 lines of the poem. How does 'only deny' in the first line of the final stanza relate to 'imagine' in the previous stanza? What do you take 'Purpose' to mean?

[*f*] Comment on the effectiveness (what is suggested and how relevant is the suggestion) of each of the following as they occur in the poem:

    (i) calm plaque of sea;
   (ii) vague-tailed;
  (iii) drifting crease of blue;
   (iv) scouring his place for some misplaced fix;
    (v) fin-thrilling;
   (vi) in a crackle of sunlight;
 (vii) hanging in streams of light.

[*g*] Is rhyme used to give poetic shape and form to this poem? If rhyme is not used for this purpose, what makes *Mackerel* a poem and not a piece of chopped-up prose?

HIGH NOON (*p* 52)

[*a*] With what is the midday sun compared? How do words like 'charges', 'arena', 'fury', and 'foe' support the comparison? Do you find this comparison a suitable one?

[*b*] What actual event is the poet describing? (From high noon to one hour later).

[*c*] Compare this poem with *The Hurricane* as a piece of description.

THE HURRICANE (*p* 53)

[a] What does the phrase 'shore of broken teeth' suggest? What other comparisons are made in describing the storm? Do they make the scene vivid for you? Explain why or why not.

[b] What do the words 'dancing', 'yelling', 'poling' suggest about the old man at 'the storm's swirling core'?

[c] Why should the fisherman feel sorrow when all storms are ended?

[d] The last four lines of the poem are separated from the first eleven. Why do you think the poet did this?

DROUGHT (*p* 54)

[a] This poem was written because the poet saw a woman who could not bear children being falsely and excessively merry at a party. What pictures of aridness, desolation, and emptiness does the poet draw on? What is the relationship between the land in the throes of drought and the woman?

[b] In what sense or senses is it 'the sunset of her time' (line 14)?

[c] What does the song or cry of the woman convey to you? What is her hope? Why does she appeal to the world rather than to an individual in the world?

[d] What mood or attitude of the poet is suggested by these comparisons:

    (i) the city/crawling south like an oil-slick (lines 4–5);
    (ii) the blackbirds . . . fallen like moths (lines 1 and 3);
    (iii) the woman like a frail apostrophe/dances palely each evening (lines 15–16)?

[e] The city 'will soon be around her ankles.' What different meanings could this have? Which meaning seems to fit best with the theme of the poem?

[f] The woman 'dances palely among the fallen blackbirds.' What does dancing there suggest about the woman's behaviour? Could the blackbirds be the people around her? If so, what is the poet suggesting about them and their lives?

SOUL ON ICE (*p* 55)

[a] What causes the horizon to tilt and whirl to a white sky?

[b] What do these tell you about the physical setting described?

    huskies; white napkins; sun's effort glows and fades; trees, white-thighed.

[c] Which of these describe the effect being conveyed by the physical setting, and why?

> picturesqueness; despair; monotony; beauty; grandeur; emptiness; desolation.

[d] A mastodon was a prehistoric creature of great weight and size and destructive power. How does its image fit into the poem? What does the sound of the word (repeated) do for the poem?

[e] What is suggested by 'pale vaudeville' and 'Characters of the Apocalypse'?

[f] Are there any valid clues in the poem to support the idea that the physical situation is being used for comparison only? (Consider, for instance, 'city's avalanche of words'; 'waiting for words'; 'thickening my tongue'; 'I can decipher nothing now'.)

[g] What is suggested by the repetition of 'Shall I'?

[h] Why is the title of the poem *Soul on Ice* rather than, say, 'Body On Ice'? In what condition are things 'on ice'?

[i] Is this poem about:

> (i) a person injured and lost in a desert of snow;
> or (ii) a person injured and lost among people?
> Into which of these interpretations does the phrase 'I am bored with stares' fit?

[j] What part, do you think, 'lost love' plays in the experience presented by the poem? Is it related to 'our pale vaudeville' and to 'the syntax of solitude'?

HISTORY LESSON (p 56)

[a] An O.B.E. (Civ. Div.) is the honour of being admitted to the Order of the British Empire (Civil Division). If you had to pick out two key lines of this poem, which would they be and why?

[b] Which of these is the poem saying, if any?

> (i) the study of British history is of no use to West Indians;
> (ii) failing examinations does not make a person a failure;
> (iii) the successful people are those who fail school examinations.

Give your reasons for your choice, or for disagreeing. If you disagree with (i), (ii), and (iii) give your own statement.

[c] What is it to 'make history'? Who did? How?

[d] Why do you think 'no surprise showed in a face'?

[e] Is the character of the teacher one that you recognise? How effective is the poet in presenting the teacher to you? What do you find most interesting in the presentation?

[*f*] The poet uses slang words—'cuss' and 'jive'—two Latin phrases, and conversational terms. What do these make the tone or mood of his voice sound like? Does the tone of the writing lessen the meaning of the poem or make it stand out more? Explain your view.

THE LESSON (*p* 57)

[*a*] Did the 'brown tobacco jar' and the headmaster's 'shiny dome' splinter? If not, what happened to make them seem to splinter?

[*b*] Why were both shame and pride felt?

[*c*] Were grief and relief felt?

[*d*] The boy cried for 'knowledge bitterer than any grief'. What knowledge?

[*e*] 'When my grief came in'. How do you imagine or interpret this?

[*f*] What does the indifference of the goldfish stand in contrast to? In what way is the indifference of the goldfish echoed?

[*g*] Whose pride is referred to in the last line? Why do you think it is described as flashing a sudden fin like a goldfish?

[*h*] How suitable is the title 'The Lesson'?

[*i*] The poem might be said to flow as easily as conversation. Does this help to make it a good poem? What other qualities contribute?

THE DUMB-SCHOOL TEACHER (*p* 58)

[*a*] Whom did this teacher teach? How does such a teacher do his work?

[*b*] What words first tell you how he made them books? What is meant by 'made them books'?

[*c*] Explain the 'silence of their chatter'.

[*d*] How do you take the phrase 'folded lips'? Why did the poet not put 'lips' in the same line as 'folded'?

[*e*] What helps to make the phrase 'grief and glory' stand out?

[*f*] What is the mood of the poem?

A LESSON FOR THIS SUNDAY (*p* 59)

[*a*] Using the clues 'lemonade', 'hammock', and 'black maid', visualise the scene in the first eight lines. What is the mood of the poet?

[b] What happens in the next fifteen lines? What exactly did the children do to the 'yellow wings'? (A clue in the first two lines tells you what 'yellow wings' are, if you did not know before.) In what way is the poet in the last six lines no longer 'idling' as he was in the first eight lines of the poem? What phrase tells you this? Why does the change take place?

[c] Do you think the children are committing a sin against the butterfly or are they having innocent fun? What do phrases like 'little surgeon' and 'prodigies' suggest about the poet's attitude to the children's actions?

[d] The poet asserts that the girl '*herself*' is 'a thing of summery light'. Why does he stress 'herself'? What else is a thing of summery light in the poem? How do (i) 'lemon frock' and 'yellow wings', and (ii) 'frail', strengthen the identification? In what way does the phrase 'maimed teetering thing' relate to the phrase 'frocks of summer torn'?

FOR PALINURUS, THE LOST HELMSMAN (*p* 60)

[a] What does a helmsman do? What happened to this helmsman? How do you know he had not been alert? In what way are the passengers also to be blamed for the catastrophe?

[b] What other relationships can you think of that are similar to the relationship between a helmsman and his passengers?

[c] Argue for or against the reading that the helmsman is a political leader.

[d] What do the last three lines tell us about the fate of this leader?

[e] Read *O Captain, My Captain* by Walt Whitman and compare it with this poem.

NOAH (*p* 61)

[a] In what way do the following help you to imagine the events in this experience of Noah, and Noah's feelings about these events:
'the waters closed like mouths over the last known hills';
'numbed . . . by horizon's drone, and the dry patter of rain';
'Noah claustrophobic sat and watched';
'Hoping, watching . . . each time barren';
'Peering eagerly about the returning hills'.

[b] What phases in Noah's experience do the following represent: 'Numbed to a stare' and 'Naming, explaining, directing'?

[c] What attitude of the poet to Noah comes out in the phrase 'sailor for the kingdom of Truth's sake'? How does this compare with the poet's attitude in the phrase 'the bearded one, the prophet, Noah', preceded as it is by the words 'nobody realised/Nothing had changed.'

[d] In the final stanza, what does 'its' refer to? What happened to it? Why does the poet use the word 'abandoned'? What mission do you think was abandoned?

[e] In line 3 we read of 'his mind's ark'. In stanza 3, the ark is described. What elements in the poem support a comparison between the ark and Noah's mind? (How, for instance, do you interpret the line 'But only animals moved in his mind'? What do 'animals' correspond to, and what attitude do you think it reveals to the things moving in Noah's mind?)

[f] Re-read stanza 3 in the light of your answers to question [e]. Does the stanza serve any other function than that of just describing the ark?

[g] 'Something he thought must come/Of this.' Did something come of it? Discuss the view that this is a poem about the failure of a man to discover the guiding principle for a new life.

COLUMBUS (p 63)

[a] Where do you imagine the action of this poem taking place? What do stanzas 1 and 2 tell you of the 'I's' attitude to this place?

[b] To the narrator's declaration that he would rather not live in the place described, Columbus replies 'But Europe never guessed America'.
What connection do you see between the two remarks?

[c] What do lines 31–32 imply about countries that have already been found? Where, then, could the 'country that cannot fail' exist?

[d] How do you interpret the phrase 'City surpassing thought'?

[e] Plato's The Republic gives his clear vision of the ideal state. What do you think the word 'glass' means in line 21? Why is it that the men in line 24 'died of despair'?

[f] What familiar word does 'sprit' look and sound like? Does the poet mean you to think about this other word too? What does it suggest about, or add to, the meaning of the poem?

[g] How would you explain the 'I's' being with Columbus to someone who does not believe in ghosts? In the end the narrator's Columbus continues on his quest but the narrator remains where he would rather not. Does he learn anything from the exchange with Columbus?

[h] Which of these, if any, can be said to be the concern of the poem:
   (i) The disillusionment of the narrator ('I');
  (ii) A view of the discoverer of America;
 (iii) A meditation on the nature of the questing spirit;
 (iv) The compromise made by the narrator?

DEATH OF A COMRADE (p 65)

[a] Which feeling is stronger in this dirge—mourning or determination? What makes you say so?

[b] What do you consider lines 19–21 to mean? Why?

[c] Can you offer an explanation of the final line? What effect does the repetition of this line have in the poem?

CORTÈGE (p 66)

[a] What is a cortège? Whose cortège is this one? Use these clues to work out whose death the poem was inspired by: 'freedom', 'black hands', 'Atlanta Street', 'South'.

[b] Is it as important to identify the particular person whose death inspired the writing of the poem as it is to imagine *the kind of person* the poet describes?

[c] What images come to mind with:
   (i) 'Feet stuttering an alphabet of faith' (Why 'alphabet'?);
  (ii) 'limp, lowered like flags';
 (iii) 'grief's wind'.

[d] What context do the words 'armour', 'weapons', and 'chariot' usually suggest? In what sense is this context appropriate to the activities of the person described? How do the words 'bronze', 'silence', and 'green farm wagon' work to modify the usual associations?

[e] What does the poet mean by referring to the South as both 'wounding' and 'sworded'? How does the word 'healed' in line 23 affect your interpretation of the word 'sworded'?

[f] Consider this arrangement of the first few lines of the poem—

> Their grief's wind blows him three and a half miles home to freedom,
> their black hands limp,
> lowered like flags,
> feet stuttering an alphabet of faith.

What are the advantages or disadvantages, in your opinion, of the poet's arrangement of the lines?

DON (*p* 67)

[*a*] Don Drummond ('The Don') was a popular Jamaican musician whose mastery of the trombone was recognised by musicians in the United States and England.
What line of the poem tells you that he is dead?

[*b*] Who is the speaker in the poem? Why do you think the poet has written the poem in the vernacular or popular speech of the country? Do you think the poem might have been a better poem if the poet had not used a colloquial style? Give your reason or reasons.

[*c*] What is the speaker of the poem praying for? 'Babylon' refers to those people regarded as corrupt. What do you take his phrase 'the evil season' (line 15) to mean?
What, would you say, 'The Don' meant to him?

[*d*] Which line or lines tell you what the poet thinks Don himself felt?

[*e*] Do any images or pictures of places come to your mind when you read the poem? If so, what associations do they arouse in you? What is the poet communicating to you by arousing these associations?

from NEW WORLD A-COMIN' (*p* 68)

[*a*] What places are named in the poem? How do these names tell you what land will not be seen for a long time?

[*b*] Who, then, are the 'we' who are leaving?

[*c*] What does the sound of the phrase 'soft, wet, slow green' suggest about the farms and the departing ones' attitudes to them?

[*d*] Who are the hard men, the cold men? What clue or clues in the poem give you the answer?

[*e*] Where are the new waters and new harbours?

[*f*] Give the substance of the lines beginning 'Our blood . . . new ancestors' in your own words.

[*g*] Would you say the poet feels any of these—joy, pride, humility, anger, sorrow, bitterness, pity, happiness, exultation, triumph? What particular phrases, words or thoughts suggest to you the feelings of the poem?

[*h*] Which of these, if any, is the poem about?
   (i) emigration
   (ii) the birth of a new nation
   (iii) suffering.
   Argue from the poem.

[*i*] Locate the following devices in the poem and comment on how they contribute to its effectiveness: alliteration, repetition, simile, metaphor and rhyme.

PAGES FROM A JOURNAL, 1834 (*p* 69)

[*a*] 'We sail at dusk'. How much does the poem tell you about the country being left? What line tells you the country being sailed for?

[*b*] Does the traveller feel regret or gladness about leaving? Refer to specific lines.

[*c*] In line 6 the poet writes 'The island *floats* behind'. Why is 'floats' better than 'stands behind' or 'lies behind'; what does the word suggest?

[*d*] Compare the poet's arrangement with this arrangement of lines 6 and 7:
> The island floats behind me
> Not leaving

What are the advantages of the poet's version?

[*e*] What is the effect of 'seaweed cord' on the way you imagine lines 8 and 9?

[*f*] What do 'printed', 'signed', 'woodcut' help to suggest about the voyager's relationship with the land and people he is about to leave?

[*g*] The poet writes 'the turning fruit prepare a tropic gold'. Would you have preferred 'the bananas ripen'? Give reasons for your choice.

[*h*] 'Sea knots', line 41, might mean (i) nautical miles (ii) the knots that tie the ship to its mooring. Using either or both of these meanings, consider the validity of the image 'Sea knots slip apart'. What contrast does the poet intend in lines 41 to 43?

KITE-FLYING (*p* 71)

[*a*] Where does the writer see a kite again? Where did he fly his bamboo kite?

[*b*] What distance has he travelled—in time or place?

[*c*] What lines tell how he feels about seeing a kite again?

[*d*] Is this poem easier to read than *A Lesson for This Sunday*? If so, why?

THE ROOM (*p* 72)

[*a*] Cezanne was an artist, an old master. What was the halfmillion Cezanne?

[*b*] Why was the room silent? Who were the 'worshippers'? What were they doing?

[*c*] What kind of atmosphere in a place can be described as 'wan'?

[d] What 'sacrilege' had to be guarded against?

[e] Did you need the poet to tell you 'like in church'? Give your reason.

[f] What do 'parody', 'bad drawing', and 'privilege' suggest to you about the writer's view of what was happening?

[g] Does the poet's voice sound mocking or reverential? Point to the clues that guide you, and tell who or what is being mocked or revered.

[h] Is the young woman the most sensible person in the room or the least appreciative of great art, according to the poet?

THE HARLEM DANCER (p 73)

[a] 'Her falsely-smiling face' (line 13). Does this mean she was deceitful and treacherous? Why was she falsely-smiling?

[b] 'I knew her self was not in that strange place'. What does this tell you about the poet's feelings about the dancer and how he wants you to feel? Why does he call the place strange?

[c] What other phrases tell you of the poet's attitude to the dancer; and which ones give you his attitude towards the other people in the place?

[d] Which of these, if any, is the poem concerned mostly with—
  (i) the beauty of the dancer;
  (ii) the suppression of coloured people;
  (iii) the degradation of human beings by the evils of the society in which they live?

[e] In what other poems in this book have you met the same kind of arrangement and form? Is there any change of thought here between the first eight lines and the last six lines?

I SHALL RETURN (p 74)

[a] Where is the poet longing to return to?

[b] What is the pain for which he wants ease?

[c] What things does he say he remembers most? Can you suggest why he says that those things are what he remembers most?

[d] Some people use the word 'native' to suggest something inferior in some way. What does the poet mean to convey when he uses it in this poem?

[e] How can tunes 'stir the hidden depths of native life'?

[f] Why does the poet describe the tunes as 'stray melodies'?

[g] Does the poem make you feel anything? If it does, describe the feeling as clearly as you can and mention the things in the poem that bring that feeling to you.

[h] Compare the rhythm of the lines and the arrangement of the rhymes with that of *The Harlem Dancer*. What do you notice?

[i] In what way does the feeling of this poem resemble that of *Pages from a Journal, 1834*, and in what way is it different?

SOUTH (*p* 75)

[a] In stanza 1 the poet describes his 'islands' bright beaches'. In which stanzas does he finish the description?

[b] 'Beaches ... lands of the north ... savannas ... forest.' Trace the journey made by the poet in stanza 2. Why does/should the forest oppress him?

[c] What is the continuous flowing of the rivers likened to by the poet? What does he imagine this flowing to reprove? What is the wisdom that is resented? In what different senses is it possible to take the word 'cunning' (line 18)?

[d] Whom do you think the poet sees as the people of the rivers, and whom as those 'born of the ocean'? What are the differences between the two groups? To which group does he belong?

[e] The river is described as having had 'pains', 'sorrows', and 'hatred', these experiences giving it certain enduring qualities. What is the river being compared to?

[f] How do stanzas 3 and 4 help you to understand why the 'I' who is 'born of the ocean' wishes to join up with 'the travelling river'?

[g] How do the 'I's' reflections on his travels help you to understand both 'Today I recapture the islands'/bright beaches' and 'the limitless morning before us'?

SQUATTER'S RITES (*p* 77)

[a] What do you glean from the poem about the 'facts' in the squatter's life: What did he do? What was his name? What happened to him?

[b] What do the words 'king', 'dignity', 'majesty', 'deposition', and 'anarchy' suggest about the second way in which the poet wishes us to see the squatter's life? What does the phrase 'parliament of *dreams*' tell us about this way of seeing the squatter's life? Whose were the dreams?

[c] How significant do you think is the difference between the life of the squatter and that of his son? What is the effect of the cliché 'dug' (referring to the son's activity) coming as it does after the description of the old man's kind of digging? Do you find any similarity between the attitudes of father and son to their own activities?

[d] What happened 'at night' when the band played 'soul'?
What suggestions does the poet build into the last nine lines?

[e] Consider the descriptive and emotional value of
  (i) 'snarled anarchy';
  (ii) 'threading the shuddered moths';
  (iii) 'leaf-white, senatorial lizards';
  (iv) 'leaning in its hole/like a sceptre'.
How do these phrases fit into the meaning of the poem?

[f] Comment on the suggestions in the title of the poem—to what extent does the poem bear out these suggestions?

ANCESTORS (p 78)

[a] What makes the poet describe his grandfather as 'black English country gentleman'?

[b] How much respect was shown for the grandfather's memory after his death? How can you judge?

[c] 'Only his hat is left'; 'Now he is dead'. What do these indicate about the poet's mood? How does this mood affect the account of what happened to the grandfather's property? What else in the stanza helps you to understand the poet's feeling about the grandfather? In the light of stanza 1, consider why the poet has chosen to tell us what happened to the horse, the trap, the wheel, and the hat.

[d] Make a mental picture of what is contained in the last line of stanza 2. What associations does this image have for you?
What part does it play in the total meaning of the stanza?

[e] What makes the rhythm in Part 3 easy to recognise? Compare the following two versions of lines 1–4 with the poet's version:

  (i) Every Friday morning my grandfather left his farm of canefields, chickens, cows, and rattled in his trap down to the harbour town to sell his meat. He was a butcher, six-foot-three and very neat.

  (ii) Every Friday morning
      My grandfather
      Left his farm
      Of canefields, chickens, cows,

And rattled in his trap
Down
To the harbour town
To sell his meat.
He was a butcher
Six-foot-three and very neat.

Which of the three versions do you prefer, and why?

WHO'S SAMMY? (p 80)

[a] What feeling does this poem communicate to you in the first
five stanzas? Can you account for how that feeling is brought
across?

[b] What makes stanza 6 stand out and bring the focus of attention
to it?

[c] How do you apprehend:
  (i) a wound apart from a stain;
  (ii) pinned to a lewd grin;
  (iii) clown's crucifixion?

OGUN (p 81)

[a] What do you see the uncle doing in the first 26 lines? Did he work
hard at it? How do you know? What phrases tell you how skilful he
was? Is he successful at his trade? If not, why not?

[b] 'There was no shock . . . couldn't handle' (lines 11–12); 'Cold
world of wood . . . whittled' (lines 15–16). What suggestions do
these sentences convey to you?

[c] How strong are bird bones? What is the difference between 'steel-
like' as against 'steel'? What then does the phrase 'hollow . . .
bones' suggest about the poet's attitude to 'what the world
preferred'? What do this and the lines quoted in question [b],
suggest about the poet's attitude to the uncle's work?

[d] What in line 27 tells you that the block of wood had not been seen
by 'the world'? What do 'on Sundays' and 'worked away' tell you
about the uncle's attitude to his work on the block of wood?

[e] The uncle's hands come to feel how the block of wood ' had
swelled and shivered, breathing air'. What does the phrase make
you imagine? What event in the life of the block of wood does the
phrase suggest? Comment now on the suggestions in 'its *weathered*
green burning to rings of *time*'. What stage in the life of the block
of wood does it make you imagine?

[*f*] The uncle's hands explore and cut their way to a crucial point. Whose hands operate in a similar way? Does line 31 help you to justify your comparison?

[*g*] What feeling about the forest is conveyed in lines 35–39? What details in these lines convey this feeling?

[*h*] *Ogun*, the title of the poem, is the name of an African god, and masks of wood are carved to represent him. Does this information locate the forest imagined in line 34? What connection do you see between the tribal makers of masks of Ogun, and the 'Uncle' in this poem?

[*i*] What is the relationship between:
  (i) the experience in lines 35–39,
  (ii) the life of the carpenter in his community (1–26), and
  (iii) the details of the carving given in lines 40–46?

ALLEGRE (*p* 83)

[*a*] What scenes and activities does the poet detail in lines 1–16? What impresses you most in the descriptions of pigeons in lines 3 and 4? Why do you suppose the shacks in line 5 are described as 'gilded'?

[*b*] Putting aside the things you do not immediately understand, what kind of feeling do you get from the set of images the poet presents? Why do you think he has used such images?

[*c*] What is the bird in lines 7–9 doing and what does this tell you about its mood? Try to see, with your mind's eye, bird's claws and then roots. Do you see any resemblance between 'claws' and 'roots'?
Consider again the bird's claws fastening round the branch on which it stands. Apart from the possible visual resemblance, how might the bird's claws be likened to roots?
What does 'of delight' suggest about the bird's sensations?
Does the claws' 'fastening round' the branches suggest anything about the bird's sensations too?
Does the comparison between the bird and 'the singer in his prime' strike you as apt? Why?

[*d*] Does the image of the bird fit in with your findings in answer to question [*b*]?

[*e*] What deficiencies in his people or country does the poet list in lines 23–26? What compensations does he find? Put the lines in your own words. What is the mood of the poet? What comment does he make on this mood?

[*f*] What is it 'to find the true self'? Why does the poet say it is arduous? Is he referring to the self of an individual or some other kind of self?

[g] Can the poem be interpreted as a reflection on the West Indian situation? How does the reference to 'young Italy' help you to think about this?

[h] What does drought bring to mind? How does the poet suggest that the loveliness might be deceptive and the elation useless? What is the unseen/unknown danger?

[i] How fitting is the title *Allegre*? What is the mood of the poem?

THE KNIFE OF DAWN (p 84)

[a] What connection do you make between 'prison' (line 2) and 'blade of fury' (line 3)? Why is the blade seen as the world's hope?

[b] In what sense would you say the 'we' are 'sweepers of an ancient sky'? What do you take 'new planets' (line 5) to mean? What dawn seems to be referred to? Why is it a sharp knife?

[c] The 'I' of the poem makes his dance 'right here' and 'on the wall of prison' but does not find it 'easy to be free.' Why do you suppose he asks the flood not to drench his feet and to subside? What flood is he addressing?

[d] In stanza 2 does the image of hope as an eagle seem clear and meaningful to you? Why, or why not? What link is there between 'hope' in line 14 and 'the heart's life' in line 21? How does the thought expressed in the final lines of the poem relate to the thoughts in the first and second stanzas?

Index of Poems by Author

Index of First Lines

Teacher's Notes

Both the compilers of this anthology and the publishers will be glad to receive comments on it and suggestions for its improvement